What others a

A Handf~~~~ ~~~~

Trésor Yenyi is a true pioneer in bringing hope, victory and grace wherever he steps. *A Handful of Rice* will fill you with courage to make a difference where change needs to come in Jesus' name. As a brother in the faith, I've seen firsthand the Father's heart through Trésor's actions to set captives free in America and the Democratic Republic of Congo.

Jeff Frost
CEO of Victory Ministry and Sports Complex., Joplin, Missouri

As I read the stories within this book, my heart swelled with joy and pride for my friend. He has been ever faithful to share the work God has done through Mwangaza with sincerity and truthfulness. His stories beautifully depict the resilience of the Congolese people, the undeniable power of relentless hope, and the abundant love of the God we serve. Trésor has said that his life's dream is to "change the world". Indeed, he is doing just that. The pages of this book depict the life-changing work he does and every captivating story will leave you encouraged and inspired.

Jenny Marrs
Host of "Diamond in the Rough" (HGTV)

Trésor has personally inspired me to be more authentic and bold in my faith. Enjoy reading the testimonies in this book. May they stretch you and encourage you to grow in your own faith and obedience to God's calling.

Mike Nichols
Lincoln Christian University

A Handful of Rice captures the heart of Trésor Yenyi beautifully. Our life experiences are one of the most important gifts that God gives to us. God has used Trésor's experiences to rebuild his own life and compel him to share that opportunity with vulnerable people across the DR Congo. The need is immense but through God, as Trésor's life reminds us, nothing is impossible!

Tom Overton
Global Director, HOPE61

Captivating, challenging, pragmatic and challenging. Such is my opinion on this revolutionary book Yenyi has just made available for the reader who aspires to learn from the best face of Africa. The leitmotif of this book lies in the fact that through the combination of small efforts, one is capable of great achievements. This is precisely what Mwangaza has continuously done for 13 years.

Pastor Gabriel Oleko
Pastor,
Regional Director of Africa, Nehemiah Project

I first met Trésor at a missions conference in Indianapolis in 2006 when he was a 23-year old sophomore in college. Our Congo journey together is a reminder that our stories belong to each other via God's divine appointments. The uniting text of John 10:16 reminds us that for those who hear the voice of the Lord, their lives will be forever transformed and I see that through Trésor's life experiences.

Duvon McGuire
President of New Life International

In his account, Trésor Yenyi rejects the pessimistic views of many authors, journalists, political analysts and even academic researchers who see only an apocalyptic future for his native country.

Trésor's life is a testimony of what must be done by his generation of Congolese in the diaspora. Following President's John Kennedy famous quote, "ask not what your country can do for you, ask what you can do for your country", Trésor has decided to serve his nation. With faith in the Holy Spirit as fuel for all his actions, Trésor is establishing himself in his home town of Kinshasa where he is helping millions of people solve everyday problems to the best of his abilities.

Barnabé Kikaya Bin Karubi
Professor, University of Kinshasa

A
Handful
of
RICE

A Congolese war survivor's story
of hope, grace, and victory

Trésor Yenyi

with Abigail Peter

NEHEMIAH
PUBLISHING

A Handful of Rice

Nehemiah Publishing
A Division of Nehemiah Project International Ministries, Inc.
5200 SW Meadows Rd, Suite 150,
Lake Oswego, OR 97035, U.S.A.
Phone: 1-877-916-1180
Fax: 503-726-5911
Printed in the U.S.A.
FIRST EDITION

Cover design and layout by Vine House Productions.
Author's picture by Mark Neuenschwander, 9Art Photography
(www.9artphoto.com)
Layout Designers: Miky Tan & Chloe Ui
Copy Editors: Roger Shipman
ISBN: 978-1-940083-24-7
Library of Congress Control Number: 2019946434

Soli Deo Gloria

Dedicated

to the victims of war

in the

Democratic Republic of the Congo

Contents

Foreword

I first met Trésor when I was a visiting lecturer at Ozark Christian College in Joplin, MO in 2006. Trésor was a student in an intensive class where I was teaching about global youth ministry. I was surprised to find out he had been born in the same city (Bukavu) in which I had served as a missionary for a decade in the Congo.

After our first conversation, I remember saying to myself, "The Lord has his hand on this young man!" I have been praying daily for Trésor and observing his life and ministry for over a dozen years now. I can testify that he has surrendered his whole heart to the Lord and that his life rings true. The stories in this book are further evidence that my initial thoughts of sensing God's favor on him were true.

While serving in the Congo, I often got discouraged with all the problems associated with extreme poverty, injustice, and political corruption. I knew in my heart the only solution to the problems of this country would be a new generation of youth who were sold out to Jesus. Trésor is a dynamic young man who gives me hope for the future of the Congo. The organization he founded, Mwangaza, is helping to raise a new generation that will bring lasting change to this country. I agree that the Congo's greatest wealth is her people and Trésor is planting seeds of hope among "the least of these."

Trésor embodies the truth of 2 Corinthians 1:3-4, "Praise be to the God and Father of our Lord Jesus Christ, the Father of compassion and the God of all comfort, who comforts us in all our troubles, so that we can comfort those in any trouble with the comfort we ourselves receive from God."

Trésor has found the deep comfort and healing he needed as a child growing up with war and continual hostility. God is now using him to pass on that same comfort to others. Trésor is living a "full-circle" life and helping others to do the same.

The name chosen by Trésor's mother seems providential. Trésor's heart breaks for the things that break God's heart. Because of that, he has become a precious treasure to many suffering children and adults in the Congo. It all started with a sense of calling and a handful of rice and now God has blessed and expanded the humble beginnings of Mwangaza, so that it now serves the most vulnerable in eight different locations across the Congo. Mwangaza has been faithful in the small things and God continues to increase its influence.

This book is full of amazing stories covered with the fingerprints of God. Fair warning, these stories may turn your world upside down. You are also going to read inspiring lessons about hope, forgiveness, healing, injustice, provision, and courage.

You will be introduced to real people who are child soldiers, orphans, street kids, AIDS victims, sex trafficking victims, rape survivors, hospital prisoners, pygmies, and children who can't afford school fees.

As Trésor and Mwangaza continue to run toward hurting people and scary things, God continues to bless and use them. Trésor and Mwangaza are shining the light of Jesus and pushing back the darkness. Proverbs 4:18 says, "But the path of the righteous is like the light of dawn, which shines brighter and brighter until full day."

Mwangaza started as a small light that continues to shine brighter and brighter every day. I pray that reading this book motivates you to add your own light and resources to this organization that is making a huge difference in the lives of hurting people.

Many have yet to discover why they have been put on earth. Trésor has clearly found his purpose in helping the most vulnerable in his home country. I pray his passion to help others will continue to spread to everyone he meets, including all who read his book. We can all learn how to love people who are hurting, let Trésor teach you.

I love hearing about all the Christian family members God continues to add to Trésor's life from different places. Since 2006, I have loved him as a son in the Lord and I am proud to be a spiritual "baba" in his life. Trésor has personally inspired me to be more authentic and bold in my faith. Enjoy reading the testimonies in this book. May they stretch you and encourage you to grow in your own faith and obedience to God's calling.

Michael Nichols, PhD
Lincoln Christian University

CHAPTER 1

Home is a place of forever wars

One morning in April 1994, at the age of eleven, I was finishing some homework in my room when my older brother Pierre barged in clutching my father's old radio in both hands.

"Listen! The rivers are running red!" he cried. There was a look of panic across his face.

Just days before, the radio had aired nonstop coverage of the assassination of Hutu supremacist Juvénal Habyarimana, the president of the Republic of Rwanda, whose plane had exploded over the airport at Kigali, the capital. That same night the Rwandan genocides began. Habyarimana's demise had set into motion a series of events that would change the course of Africa's history forever.

My parents, our relatives, and the neighbors—everyone around—spent every free minute talking about an impending war for weeks on end, but as soon as they saw us listening, they immediately changed the subject. The adults did their best to make us feel safe, but we were attentive enough to pick up on their vibrations; it made us feel cold and nervous.

It never occurred to me that in a land right next to Congo, the place I called home, ethnic Hutu supremacists had begun an extermination campaign to wipe every last Tutsi from the face of the earth.

Listening to the radio reports of the genocide with Pierre that morning in our tiny shared bedroom in Kinshasa, I still had not truly grasped how extreme the Rwandan genocide was. It never occurred to me that in a land right next to Congo, the place I called home, ethnic Hutu supremacists had begun an extermination campaign to wipe every last Tutsi from the face of the earth. Hundreds of thousands of Rwandans took to the streets and participated in mass killings in the name of ethnic cleansing. The killings were low-tech—mostly done with machetes and clubs—but were carried out with dazzling speed. In six weeks, about a million people, including 70% of the entire Tutsi population, were slaughtered in cold blood.

Pierre was right. As thousands of massacred bodies were dumped into the Kagera River, the rivers that flowed down from the hills of Rwanda into Lake Victoria did indeed turn a shocking red.

"Cook the fish thoroughly," I heard my father remind my mother as she prepared our meals, "the Ministry of Health have issued warnings; our rivers are all polluted."

Bloated and mutilated corpses were washed through our rivers. Uganda, on the northern shore of Africa's greatest lake, Victoria, declared three of its districts disaster areas: the bodies that had washed ashore glutted its waters. They had to appeal for international help to dispose of the bodies. As I listened, I imagined peasant fishermen working together with international humanitarian workers, picking out these corpses, and dutifully counting the number of bodies retrieved for the day: 18, 19, 20, ..., while the bloody, rotting stench of dead bodies filled the air and permeated their senses.

But far worse than the stench of corpses that had filled the air in the region was a stronger wave that was making people lose their senses: the horrible and dangerous stench of hatred that began to infiltrate the regions around Rwanda.

Though I did not quite grasp the enormity of genocide, as a Congolese boy, I understood perfectly well the pain, loss, and violence that were associated with war. My mother, a good storyteller, often told us of the wars she had experienced during her childhood in Kisangani. She narrated so vividly that we would feel transported to the very moment the rebel troops invaded Kisangani in the 1970s.

Stories have a way of shaping impressions. My mother's stories left me with an impression that death can arrive at any moment and in many forms—it starts with hate and ends with guns, machetes, disease, and hunger.

Congo had been mired in conflict for decades. From the very moment Patrice Lumumba, Congo's first Prime Minister took to the stage on its independence day, June 30, 1960, and delivered one of the greatest speeches of the twentieth century, many believed that Congo was damned.

In his speech, Lumumba publicly denounced colonialism and affronted Belgium and King Baudouin personally. The Belgian government and Lumumba's opposers associated his revolutionary and bold ways with communism. They spread rumors that Lumumba had been bought by the communists. His fateful speech was believed to be one of the contributing factors that led to his assassination a short six months later. His successor Mobutu Sese Seko seized power in a military coup and named himself president. Thus began Mobutu's 30-year long dictatorship over the people and lands of Congo.

Death can arrive at any moment and in many forms—it starts with hate and ends with guns, machetes, disease, and hunger.

My mother always reminded me of the time when Western names were outlawed in Congo. "I still knew you had to be named Trésor, even if we could have been in trouble with certain authorities because of your name. I knew you had to be called treasure," she said with pride.

As part of Mobutu's campaign to enforce an "African cultural awareness," he ordered all Congolese with Christian names to drop them and change to African ones. The baptism of children was outlawed, and western-style clothing banned. The Democratic Republic of the Congo became the Republic of Zaire and Joseph Mobutu changed his name to Mobutu Sese Seko Kuku Ngbendu Wa Za Banga, which means "The all-powerful warrior who, because of his endurance and inflexible will to win, will go from conquest to conquest, leaving fire in his wake."

The people's minds, Mobutu felt, had been bent beneath colonialization for too long. His plan was to liberate them mentally as well. A host of name changes would help in that process. Leopoldville became Kinshasa, Stanleyville became Kisangani, and Elizabethville became Lubumbashi.

During his thirty-year reign he would amass a fortune of over $5 billion while the average citizen in his country would eke out a mere $200 annual income. Revolt was consistent throughout Mobutu's reign, but it was generally suppressed. Only after the Rwandan genocide did tensions rise to an all-time high, and an already unstable Zaire plunged into a further catastrophic mess.

In July 1994, one hundred days after the genocide began, The Rwandan Patriotic Front (RPF), consisting of massed Tutsis, captured Kigali, Rwanda's administrative capital. The government collapsed, and tides of Rwandan Hutu refugees fled their homes, fearing retribution from the new military forces for perpetrating the genocide. They fled into the bordering regions of Zaire and Tanzania—approximately two million of them to be precise—creating one of the largest movements of refugees in modern world history.

Meanwhile, in Kinshasa, Zaire's administrative capital, a new leader emerged from the bloody throes of the genocide. Laurent-Désiré Kabila was a robust figure, a man with meat on his bones, who laughed broadly and exuded an air of ease, even nonchalance. In October 1996, the Alliance des Forces Démocratiques Pour La Libération (AFDL) was set up. Kabila was its official spokesperson and received the honorable term of address *Mzee*, which in Swahili means elder.

The Alliance was a coalition of Rwandan, Ugandan, Burundian and selected Congolese dissidents. In other words, the alliance was made up of ethnic Tutsis who had lived in Zaire for generations but was growing precarious due to the sudden migration of hundreds and thousands of ethnic Hutus settling into refugee camps across Zaire.

9

"Everything will be different now that we are getting rid of the vieux leopard [old leopard],"

Kabila would address crowds of thousands during grand rallies, promising the people that the refugees would return to Rwanda where they belonged. With that, the AFDL began capturing towns along the Zairean border to disperse the large Hutu refugee camps. Thousands of these refugees died of starvation and vicious attacks as the AFDL used violence to carry out mass atrocities during this period. Despite the violence, they won the support of the people, who at this point were weary of Mobutu's thirty-two-year dictatorship.

"Everything will be different now that we are getting rid of the *vieux leopard* [old leopard]," Kabila promised the people. He told overblown stories of his liberation army and urged parents to donate a child to support the cause. His charisma was undeniable. He was a breath of fresh air.

I was shocked to see the faces of these soldiers: mere children in plastic boots and camouflage outfits.

The AFDL first pressed through the three most important cities in Congo—Uvira, Bukavu and Goma. It took them seven months. However, in 1997, with foreign help and the blessing of the United States, they propelled across Zaire almost unopposed, arrived in Kinshasa right in my neighborhood, and ended Mobutu's thirty-two-year reign. Zaire was renamed the Democratic Republic of the Congo.

On the day the rebel troops marched into Kinshasa in their Wellington boots and rifles, I truly saw the horrors the fires of war produce. Most of the city's population celebrated the victory that ended thirty-two years of dictatorship; crowds flooded the streets of Kinshasa to celebrate their liberators. I was shocked to see the faces of these soldiers: mere children in plastic boots and camouflage outfits. My heart broke for them, holding guns sometimes as tall as they were. But the crowds around me were cheering; to them they were heroic, fearless children fighting for their country.

The troops systematically laid siege to the city. First, they took over the Inga Dam, a large hydroelectric dam 250km southwest of Kinshasa that directly supplied its electricity. The entire city was without power for two weeks. Then they cut off food and water supplies. Everybody hid out in their houses. Kinshasa's population at that time was estimated to be about six million people. There was no sugar, no salt, no beer, hardly any cassava—nobody could go out to the fields. It was a time when people really got to know about hunger. Babies died in hospitals, and despair spread through the city. The punishment for fighting back was to be burned in public by AFDL troops.

I stayed indoors for the most part, relying on the radio for news from the outside. Occasionally my father's friends came by our home. My uncle Gaston, an imposing six-footer with large hands and broad shoulders, brought us news from the hospital where he worked. This often came as respite from the constant radio reports we obsessively listened to. "There are tens of thousands of people dying from cholera in Goma. We're actually better being out here in Kinshasa."

"Thank God," I heard my mother say.

Maman's response was shocking and it deeply troubled me. How could anyone be thankful for all that has come upon us, I wondered. Could Goma really be in a worse state then Kinshasa? What could be worse than this? Even if there were tens of thousands dying of cholera on the desolate volcanic region around Goma, even if mass graves were filled with women, children, and the elderly under a sky darkened by ash spewing from a rumbling volcano, Kinshasa was in no way a better place to be for anyone.

My town was in tatters. Neighbors turned on neighbors. My church and school were now slaughterhouses rather than safehouses. Kinshasa was such a big part of my life and, despite the spoils of the war; I loved it in the unconditional way that a child will forever love their first home. I simply could not comprehend why life could never be the same again for us in Kinshasa.

No matter how many times my father consoled us children by saying that this was only a temporary situation—and I think he truly believed that—I was growing hostile; there seemed to be no end to the war. There will always be a new rebellion or a new battle, and now, because of them, I had to watch my home as I knew it fall apart.

CHAPTER 2

These hard times will pass

When I was a little boy, my siblings and I would gather around to listen to stories that my grandmother would animatedly share with us. She had many stories to tell and as a young boy, I believed them all. "Before God created people, He prepared many gifts of nature and put them all in a basket. Then he went to the different regions around the world and distributed these gifts. At the end, when God arrived in Congo, he was exhausted and decided to stop and rest. While he lay resting, he decided that He would leave all the remaining gifts in the basket in Congo." Her eyes would light up every time she reached this part of the story. "Before God made people, Congo was the richest country on earth."

Before God made people, Congo was the richest country on earth.

A land with limitless water from the world's second-largest river—the Congo—a benign climate, and rich soil, Congo was beautiful. Beneath the abundant and fertile ground sit copious amounts of copper, gold, diamonds, cobalt, coltan, uranium and oil—just some of the minerals that should in fact make it one of the world's richest countries today. Congo truly is a land seemingly blessed with every type of mineral of the earth. Every time I remembered Grandmother's story I would look out to the hills, swell with pride, and thank God for his gifts. But today was different.

Today, I just wanted to drown out the sounds of war and fall into a deep sleep. I closed the windows in my room, a habit I had acquired over the last few months, mainly to ensure the stray bullets fired by the rebel forces did not find their way into my room. As I lay on my bed, staring at the ceiling, I heard the mayor's speech over the radio in the living room. "Rest assured that under our new government, Congo will now thrive, and the people will prosper."

Pierre's commentary soon followed, "I hear he's

killed a few Hutu refugees himself, too."

I shut my eyes but could still hear the sounds going off in my head. Shots being fired, people screaming and crying. I tossed and turned to find a comfortable spot on my bed. It had been a struggle to fall asleep over the past few months. I kept my eyes closed and tried so hard to lose my thoughts. Soon enough I slowly drifted away before I heard a deep but firm voice speaking. It was our minister.

□   □   □

"And this water symbolizes baptism that will now also save you. It saves you by the resurrection of Jesus Christ." And with that I watched the parish minister submerge my little brother Deo backward into the banks of Congo River just west of Kinshasa.

The bright light of the sun was shining as Deo stood in the river, his brand new linen white shirt completely soaked. Everyone was applauding. I took a deep breath and smelled the salt in the air. I looked around and saw glorious hills surrounding the vast volumes of water. There were people watching us from the shore, standing on the rocks. Some were washing clothes, some were hauling water. But mostly everyone was in high spirits.

As Deo rose out of the water that afternoon, he looked like a brand new person—completely different. That was the very first moment in my life where I saw how the Holy Spirit could have His way in every person's life. I would experience a few such moments in the future, but that was the first, the significant moment where I began to believe that a new heart is a dramatic declaration of God's power to heal, deliver and fix brokenness. The minister preached that afternoon on the importance of water baptism. "Water baptism has been purchased for us through the most expensive price ever paid: the blood of Jesus. There is no element in the world more expensive. You can pile up all the gold, diamonds, emeralds, pearls, all the financial empires of the world; put them on one side, put a drop of the blood of Jesus on the other side and ask, "Which is more powerful?" and there is no comparison. One drop of the blood of Jesus can save us all."

Deo's baptismal celebration continued at our home with our friends and family. It was also the day that Deo's and my favorite soccer team was playing in the finals of the African Champions League. My mother had specially prepared a feast to celebrate Deo. There was plenty of cassava and my favorite grilled fish dish, Pondu. She specifically added extra green peppers for a flavor-filled fiesta, because she knew that is how I liked it. No one grills fish the way Maman does, I thought, as I scooped up a huge portion to fill my plate.

There was Congolese Rumba music playing through the radio, but my attention was fixated on the screen as I watched Zamalek take on the Nigerian Shooting Stars. They were closing in on the first half when Zamalek shot their second goal. "GOAL!" I heard Deo shout. Our favorite team was in the lead now. I picked up a handful of rice from my plate, ready to feed myself, and in that moment, I felt satisfied, as if a wee bit of heaven drifted right there in my home. Not only was my hand full of rice, it was overflowing, and my heart was full of joy and my life in that moment was perfect.

□   □   □

> Not only was my hand full of rice, it was overflowing, and my heart was full of joy and my life in that moment was perfect.

I was rudely awakened by the sudden sweltering heat that had filled my room. My sweat-soaked skin slowly called me back to the lighter realms of wakefulness. The electricity had been cut off again. This was beginning to be a common thing; I was not used to living this way. Kinshasa was now known as the "Dark City" for its frequent power outages. Walking in the streets at night was perilous: there were no lights, and the silence was sometimes suddenly pierced by yells or laughter from the troops. Occasionally we heard the sounds of gunfire as well. But despite the hellish aspects of life in Kinshasa, it still occupied a treasured place in my heart, for I had such fond memories of life here before the war.

Before the troops invaded Kinshasa, our neighborhood streets were lush and green, heavily scented with trees laden with mangoes and papayas. The city gleamed with white buildings and broad, nearly empty streets. Best of all, the city was crime free.

It was the year 1974, and Mobutu had offered a whopping $10 million to draw international attention to Kinshasa as they hosted the "Rumble in the Jungle," a legendary boxing event that saw Muhammad Ali and George Foreman slug it out for the world heavyweight title. Zaire was on the world map, the world was watching, and Mobutu wanted the streets crime free. He allegedly rounded up 1,000 of Kinshasa's most notorious criminals before the fight and held them in rooms under the stadium before executing 100 of them to enforce his point. Unsurprisingly, the city was virtually crime-free for quite some time after the event.

Everyone seemed to have fond memories of Kinshasa before the war. It felt as if that were a long time back.

Sometimes when Father's business friends would come over, they would reflect upon these times with fondness. I would hover around them silently and listen. Everyone seemed to have fond memories of Kinshasa before the war. It felt as if that were a long time back.

I took a deep breath, fumbled with my blanket, got out of bed, and slowly made my way out of my room to the kitchen to fetch a glass of water. In the dark stillness, I could not see much but could tell that the

Maman was equally at ease as both a refined woman of sophisticated tastes, yet at the same time every bit an African village woman.

time was past midnight. The authorities had ordered a curfew to keep the situation under control. Every now and then, we could hear the sound of the troops making their rounds, speaking in crass Swahili, most of them usually drunk by nightfall. None were making their rounds tonight; a deafening silence reigned.

The kitchen was well lit. I saw Maman had set up two candles on top of the sugar jars. Her head was bowed; her Bible lay next to her. Maman was an intelligent woman. She was raised in Kisangani; as a result, her perspective on life differed from many that were raised in the city of Kinshasa. She was an expert at writing precise, flowery scripts for our church plays. She knew how to do dainty needlepoint stitch work and was the best at cooking traditional Lokele dishes. Maman was equally at ease as both a refined woman of sophisticated tastes, yet at the same time every bit an African village woman.

The garden in our home when we lived in Lubumbashi was always full of roses and fruit trees. Maman was very good with her hands, and she loved gardening. The heady scent of roses greeted you as you walked into our compound. Maman loved nothing more than puttering in the garden, tending to our lush and beautiful fruit trees. Not everyone had fruit trees in our neighborhood—ours sometimes produced fruits as big as our heads.

After we moved to Kinshasa, our compound was smaller and tighter, but Maman showed us that you didn't need a huge plot to create a beautiful compound. She maximized whatever space we had and beautified our tiny porch with colored pots and blooming flowers.

She heard me rummaging around in the kitchen and looked up. "Trésor, dear, is there something you need?"

"Yes, just water," I replied abruptly. I saw that she had been crying.

The past few months had been hard on all of us, but Maman was a strong woman. She had, after all, lived through a war before. I had never seen Maman cry.

"Do you remember your Uncle Henri and Aunty Bernadette? They are no more. They were killed by rebels that looted their home. I just received the news last night."

Her voice shook as she spoke. Her favorite brother and his family had been killed. I could not imagine the pain Maman was experiencing. Yet there was nothing she could do.

"How could you still be grateful to God after everything that has happened to us? You said it that day when you were speaking to Uncle Gaston. You said, thank God the situation here isn't as bad as Goma. How could you still be thankful to God? It seems like God has chosen to close his eyes and ears for all of us here in Congo." I could feel my voice cracking, but it wasn't sadness this time, just anger that had been building within me for some time now.

The roots of deep hatred were rapidly spreading, like a contagious epidemic, across the Democratic Republic of the Congo, destroying and poisoning the minds of masses of people. I wish I could say that I, Trésor Yenyi, was immune to it. But I was starting to feel entitled to hate those different from

Her favorite brother and his family had been killed. I could not imagine the pain Maman was experiencing. Yet there was nothing she could do.

People of other tribes had killed, raped, and kidnapped members of my family, and I justified my hate toward them because of what they had done.

me, anyone from another tribe. Deep in my heart I felt the loss and grief of war. People of other tribes had killed, raped, and kidnapped members of my family, and I justified my hate toward them because of what they had done. In my eyes, they deserved no mercy, because they had given none.

Maman's voice remained calm, in total contrast to the bitterness, anger, and hatred that gushed out of my clenched mouth as I spoke to her. She told me that "as Christians, we have been taught to see the beauty even in the pains of war. It is in the beautiful exchange of our pain for God's love that we learn to surrender our lives to Him. Only then will we surely see the grains of rice in our hands grow, multiply and overflow.

"One day, we will realize that our lives are so full, both our hands won't be enough to hold what God has blessed us with. When that moment takes place, we would be blessed enough to give to others just as we have received. These are hard times, but someday this too will pass. But remember this, my dear Trésor, forgiveness is one of the greatest gifts that you can give yourself, for it sets you free."

forgiveness is one of the greatest gifts that you can give yourself, for it sets you free.

Maman had no idea what she was talking about, I thought. She did not know what she was saying. All I could see was that suddenly my hands were bare. The grains of rice that was once overflowing, were now slipping fast through my fingers. I was empty.

CHAPTER 3

At the crossroads of grief and love

Before the troops invaded Kinshasa, I spent my childhood years in carefree oblivion in the outdoors, riding my bicycle around the neighborhood, sometimes even all the way up to town.

We must only trust those that look and speak like us, no one else.

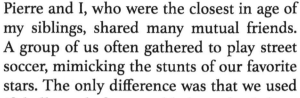

Pierre and I, who were the closest in age of my siblings, shared many mutual friends. A group of us often gathered to play street soccer, mimicking the stunts of our favorite stars. The only difference was that we used makeshift balls made from wadded-up plastic bags tied with rubber bands. It cost us nothing to make these, and kicking them around felt like kicking a real football, so we happily stuck with it for a couple of years.

Others will only pose as people in order to try to deprive us of what God meant for us to have.

By the time we were old enough to tell the difference, Congo was already deeply embroiled in a state of war. Not only did we lose our freedom to play soccer on the streets, we also saw friendships around us falter and come to an end. The kids that stopped playing with us probably never did understand why they had to sever ties with their friends. I pictured their parents repeatedly cautioning them against mingling with kids from other tribes. "We must only trust those that look and speak like us, no one else." It was events like these that further increased my hostility towards others. It seemed like everyone had a group they belonged to and each was powerfully bound to their groups.

It was as if everything boiled down to mine, mine, mine. That was both the curse and power of human beings. What we have we can share but only with people of our own. We are the real people, everyone else is an imposter. Others will only pose as people in order to try to deprive us of what God meant for us to have. Others will always be a threat. Such mindsets are dangerously contagious, especially to simple-minded young children exposed to them.

Despite the looming dark cloud of hatred in Kinshasa, my father insisted we continue going to school. It was important to him that both the boys and the girls in our family get an equally good education, which was very forward thinking of him in a community where the traditional role for girls was to marry and produce children.

School was also the only place we could actually let loose and be the children that we were. Everywhere else was unsafe, especially for young boys. The AFDL were actively recruiting child soldiers and many young boys in Kinshasa were going missing.

One day after a game of soccer in our school field, I had an interesting conversation with a good friend I will never forget. Everyone called him Beenzu, which means "visitors" in the Chitonga language of Zambia and Zimbabwe. He was quite an interesting character; always jovial and sometimes quite the prankster, he was able to take any situation and make a joke of it.

As we sat resting under a tiny shed at the corner of the field, Beenzu looked low-spirited, which was very unlike him. He told me that his father's family in Rwanda had been killed in the genocide.

I had been told on countless occasions that to hate was wrong, but now I felt that the perpetrators needed to pay the price for what they'd done.

"I will never see my cousins again." His head fell on his chest as he spoke.

I could instantly identify with Beenzu's loss. I had lost my family, too. They had been kidnapped, raped, and killed, and I was grieving their loss. Grief can come in many forms and mine came first in the form of anger. Deep, seething anger. I had been told

23

on countless occasions that to hate was wrong, but now I felt that the perpetrators needed to pay the price for what they'd done. They were violent, merciless people. Within me so much hatred was building, I told Beenzu I would never look at a Tutsi the same way again.

Beenzu, being himself, made a lighthearted remark: "It may be that God sends you a friend from Rwanda, perhaps then you might change your mind. From what I've seen and heard over the last few months, anything can happen, to anyone. It's all God's will."

"After everything that's happened to us, I'm sure God will understand if I never look into the eye of another person from another tribe. I'm sure God knows what pain they've caused us. He has to understand why I hate them."

"Don't be too sure. Someday you might be sharing your food, maybe even your home, with a Rwandan! What if God decides to make you one of those examples so the rest of us can do the same?"

There was a brief moment of silence between us before Beenzu burst into a fit of laughter after he realized what he just said sounded almost ridiculous. I had made my stance clear: I did not want to be around anyone from another tribe. What? Embrace them? NO, not a chance

Looking back now, I am sure God had been listening in on our conversation that day on the street. Because what I thought was impossible was about to become a reality. God had something planned for me. My story of grace was about to begin at the crossroads of grief and love.

CHAPTER 4

Walking into my destiny

Three years after I completed my high school education in Congo, I received a grant to study at Ozark Christian College, a small college in Joplin, Missouri. When I submitted my application, I had little hope that my application would go through, yet something inside me was at peace. It felt like the right thing to do. When I received the news that I was awarded the grant, I understood that the sense of peace I had felt was my heart prompting me to walk right into my destiny.

I was once told that when you pursue something that is meant for you, everything will naturally fall into place. Obstacles will be cleared out, and pathways will be paved for you to begin your journey. Receiving the grant gave me the conviction that going to America was going to be an easy process, regardless of what the political climate in Congo might have been at that point.

In 2004, two whole years after Laurent-Désiré Kabila was assassinated, by unanimous vote of the Congolese parliament, his son Joseph Kabila was sworn in as president to replace him. A year later, Joseph Kabila signed a peace deal with Rwanda in which he was to disarm the Hutu extremists that were causing violence, rapes, and atrocities in eastern Congo; in return, Rwanda would withdraw its remaining troops in Congo.

Despite these peace deals, fighting and appalling attacks on civilians by rebels were still occurring in eastern Congo. These recurring conflicts quickly escalated into full-scale war involving the armed forces of six African countries, including Angola, Zimbabwe, and Namibia, which intervened to support Kabila.

With Africa facing severe conflict and instability, throngs of Africans were looking to leave their home countries to pursue a different, more stable life for themselves and their families in countries like the U.S. This complicated American visa applications and made them nearly impossible to obtain. Yet I submitted my application, fully confident that I had a solid purpose and invitation to travel to America. A few weeks later, I received a call from the American embassy in Kinshasa. My application was rejected, and they gave no reason.

The rejection caught me off-guard. I thought I did everything right. A very kind lady at the embassy told me that I should not take the rejection too negatively. "It's just a lesson, so you can better yourself on your next application," she said. But I felt hopeless. That day, I walked out of the embassy with my head down, feeling dazed and rejected. I was convinced my rejection boiled down to one truth. I am a passport holder of a third-world country and getting to America is a dream that was simply too far-fetched for someone like me.

But I re-applied anyway. This time I followed specific guidelines that the kind lady at the embassy gave me. Looking back now I know that she was godsend. God always positions people in our lives to help us carry out His will.

I prayed that if it was God's will for me to go to America, he would make it happen. A week later the embassy called to inform me that my visa had been approved. This was the first of many tiny miracles that I was to experience throughout my journey. I was finally going to America, the land I had only read about in books and watched on TV.

I am a passport holder of a third-world country and getting to America is a dream that was simply too far-fetched for someone like me.

I was also finally prepared to move out of my comfort zone, to be challenged, now more than ever. As strange as it sounds, I had a deep apprehension to be discomfited by challenging new experiences.

Many of us spend our entire lives in the same bubble. We surround ourselves with those that share our opinions, speak the same languages, and look the way that we do. We fear leaving what's familiar, but only by exploring the unfamiliar can we discover what and who we are.

In the days leading up to my departure, I scribbled in my journal, "The experience of a lifetime awaits me.... I'm going to leave everything behind, my comforts, my family and my dear friends. I don't know how this will affect me, but I know at the end of my journey, I will be a changed man." Self-discovery begins where your comfort zone ends, and mine was about to end far more quickly than I had anticipated.

It was the morning of August 9, 2004, a day that will forever be etched in my memory, the day I left DRC for the very first time. I sat in the living room of my parents' house with my family, with two hours left to get to the airport, when my father began to sing a traditional French hymn that said, "Lord, take care of me. I need you. I am nothing, alone, and you know that well." My father always sang with a voice of an angel. He was well known in his hometown for leading the choir in his church. I felt comfort in hearing him sing.

Looking around the room, I noticed that everyone was praying. For me. In that profound moment I knew my life would never be the same again. Something life-changing was about to happen to me. The thought that I would no longer see my mother every morning as she prepared my breakfast or that I would not have the company of my brothers and sisters from whom I had never been separated was overwhelming. I began to cry. I don't remember feeling that sad at any point in my life. Fulfilling God's will in my life came at great personal cost: leaving my beloved family and embarking on an adventure without knowing what the future held for me.

Walking out to the front gate, I turned around and

my eyes rested on my home. The houses in Kinshasa have fences made of cement block; a front gate provides entrance to the compound. All my happiness up to that day was associated with that house; it was my entire life. I did not know any different. Little did I know that the future I was walking toward would not compare in any way to the past I was leaving behind.

I cried all the way to the airport. My father waited with me until it was time to board the plane. He didn't say much. The silence of the heart between a parent and their child is not a lonely one. My father and I did not talk much, but we did not need to. I never doubted his love or questioned his support, and today was one of those days that further reassured me of the special bond we had.

Passengers from my flight were called to cross the little doorway that led to the runway. Halfway to the plane I looked back. My father and my childhood friend were standing and waving goodbye. I waved back, turned around, and walked forward into my destiny. I left Congo equipped with the promises of Mark 10: 29-31. I trusted that God would bless me with a hundredfold as I chose to follow him.

About fifteen hours later, we landed at John F. Kennedy International Airport. The captain announced that New York was just entering fall season and the outside temperature was in the low- to mid-80s Fahrenheit. I was supposed to take a connecting flight to Missouri International Airport, and from there travel by car to my final destination in Joplin. As I made my way toward the connecting gate for my next flight, I saw an escalator for the first time. *An actual moving, automated staircase*, I thought to myself, *how fascinating*. The airport was swarming with so many people. I didn't think I'd ever seen so many moving around in one space. Most of their faces were white, with just a few black- and brown-skinned people among them. Everybody looked affluent and well-dressed, everyone was hurrying, and nobody smiled.

There was a huge floor-to-ceiling window pane that overlooked the outside of the airport. Through the window I saw lots of big buildings that looked strong enough to withstand an earthquake or even a volcano, that sometimes erupted in Goma. I remembered the stories about America that I had heard from my father's business friends, stories of buildings so tall you could not see the tops, of crowds of people speaking languages you had never heard of, of sleek motorcars and beautiful women and dashing men. Walking through JFK reminded me of these stories. I felt like I had just been flung into the center of a stream whose current I could not resist. There was a strong sense of awe and bewilderment.

When I reached the departure gate, an immigration official at the entrance asked me for my passport. Upon seeing my passport, he asked me what my purpose of travel to America was. I told him that I was here to study and handed over a file containing all my student documentation. I mentally said a quick prayer and hoped that I had all the right paperwork. After a few short moments he asked me, "What are you going to study?"

> Buildings so tall you could not see the tops, of crowds of people speaking languages you had never heard of, of sleek motorcars and beautiful women and dashing men.

I casually replied, "Biblical studies." He looked over his spectacles and sternly asked me to repeat that again.

"Biblical studies." I pronounced the words slightly slower this time, nervous like a child about to get reprimanded by the teacher for his wrongdoing. It took him some time, but I assumed everything went well when the official returned my documents with a smile and said, "Welcome to America. I hope you brought some warm clothes with you. It's going to get very cold soon."

CHAPTER 5

Forgiveness will liberate your soul

Settling in Bible college was not all that easy. My first few semesters at Ozark were some of the hardest times of my life. I felt lonely and isolated, and my meager English skills did not help. Yet, in a sense, it was also a relief to be able to start over. For the first time in my life, I was around people who knew nothing of the horrors I had witnessed. These people did not carry the same wounds I did.

But the thing that fascinated me the most was seeing how different people from so many parts of the world, that looked so different from one another, lived alongside each other peacefully without fighting or arguing.

Every day I found myself fascinated by new discoveries. As I sat on the bus, I was amazed by how organized everything was. Roads were well-built, and everyone followed the traffic rules. Joplin was not like New York. I noticed there were far fewer people and far fewer buildings, mostly just wide-open green fields. The air was crisp and fresh, and I enjoyed taking walks to do my chores and to attend my classes.

But the thing that fascinated me the most was seeing how different people from so many parts of the world, that looked so different from one another, lived alongside each other peacefully without fighting or arguing. Another favorite thing about moving to America was being able to go to bed with my windows left open. I did not have to worry about stray bullets finding their way into my room here.

One day, I went to a prayer meeting for Christian international students at a university in Springfield, Missouri. As we were fellowshipping together, I noticed a man with facial features that were very distinctively Tutsi. We were assigned to the same prayer circle, so I decided to ask him where he was from, just to confirm my initial guess. I did not even ask him his name. I just had to know where he was from.

He told me he was from Rwanda and went on to explain which part specifically. I had so much pent-up anger toward everyone from Rwanda, I instantly felt a surge of negative energy take over my thoughts. When we were asked to pray for one another in our small group session, I could not piece my thoughts together to pray for the wellness of this man.

I wondered how many members of his family may have murdered and hurt members of my family. They were all the same, I thought. It was like a volcano boiling within me. I just uttered some words and made a quick few references to him in a quick, insecure prayer. My heart wasn't in it at all.

I returned to Joplin sad and disappointed at myself, knowing that I had to deal with all the pent-up bitterness I harbored. I could not live like this forever. My time at Ozark had broadened my horizons, yet it had not broadened my mind. I was still not the entirely open-minded, unprejudiced young man I ought to be.

Two days later, the man called me. He introduced himself, and I felt a chill run up my spine. I had no idea how he got my number. He told me he needed prayer. "I believe that because we had been through the same pains and hardships in our lives, we can help bring peace in one another's life. Our friendship could be an example to many," he said.

Our friendship? I was silent for what seemed like ages. Never had I had a Rwandese friend.

"Would you prefer if we meet up for a chat?" he asked, breaking the awkward silence.

I could hardly believe my ears: his boldness utterly

astonished me. Yet at the same time it aroused and motivated me to begin to alter my perception of him.

"Uh, yes, okay, we can meet."

In a café two days later, we were talking about our families and journeys through the war, both of us dealing with the pain from its aftermath.

"You know, I never truly believed all that stuff about hatred between Hutus and Tutsis. I never hated Hutus, and I'm sure you never hated the Tutsis. You and I are just two ordinary human beings who wished nothing bad to happen to anyone else. Both of us were victims, in different ways, of evil meddlers. We were brainwashed just like many others out there."

You and I are just two ordinary human beings who wished nothing bad to happen to anyone else. Both of us were victims, in different ways, of evil meddlers.

His words struck me like a comet streaking through the night sky.

I left our meeting that day feeling lighter than I had felt for years. We had lived through the horror of a genocide and war, and while many people are appalled by it, they will never fully understand how difficult it is to fully move on. What we've witnessed, I realized, will haunt us for the rest of our lives, but forgiveness was an important process for us. A process I was still going through, a process of trying to trust and to love again.

In the coming weeks, we went around the streets of Springfield evangelizing and sharing God's word and love with the people in that area. People asked us if we were brothers. I felt proud to say yes, he was my brother because of the blood and unfailing love of Jesus Christ.

□   □   □

Just over a year since my arrival in America I found

myself experiencing another divine intervention in my life. I was in Indiana to attend an African student Christian meeting and decided to pay my dear friends Ian and Katy a visit.

I met Katy through Facebook shortly after I moved to America. We connected over our shared interest in traditional Congolese cuisine. People would often ask me the one thing about Congo that I truly missed. The answer was easy; it was Maman's tasty cooking. After some time, I figured the only way to cure my longing for Maman's traditional dishes was to actually start cooking them myself.

"Pay attention," Maman would say during our impromptu cooking lessons back in Kinshasa. "Even men must learn to cook; you can't always expect a woman to do everything. Someday you'll need to know this."

Oh, Maman, did you always have to be right about everything?

Even if the dishes I cooked did not always taste quite the same, just the smell and sight of it was good enough to nourish my soul as much as it filled my stomach. In an attempt to keep a record of the dishes I cooked, I would share pictures of the dishes I cooked on Facebook. Meanwhile, Kathy, all the way over in Indiana, had been valiantly searching for traditional Congolese recipes online. She and her husband Ian had adopted two boys from Congo. She was determined to help them ease into their new lives in the best way possible: to cook their favorite foods. She stumbled across my food posts on Facebook and with that began a wonderful friendship that I would cherish today.

Katy was thrilled when I told her I would be in Indiana for a meeting. "You must come by our home and cook something for us as well," she said. Her invitation seemed like the usual gesture any friend would make but looking back now I can see that God had already set in motion His grand plan for me.

After spending some quality time with Ian, Kathy, and their children, we made our way to the grocery store to buy the ingredients for our dinner. On the way, Ian mentioned that he had invited a pastor he knew to join our gathering. "He's actually from DRC itself, and I figured you might like to meet him. You'll be able to catch up with someone from home at the same time. He will be joining us with his family."

Immediately I felt slightly uneasy. Ever since my arrival in America, I noticed, I did not fancy meeting anyone from back home. America was meant to be a fresh start for me. Congo was home, but there were too many bitter memories in Congo. Sometimes when I try to recall a time before the war, I struggle— the events were so significant, they are ingrained in my memory for life. Meeting someone from Congo would only mean I'd have to talk about my life there, which mostly just brought me despair.

"Which part of Congo is he from?" I asked. I was trying to figure out which tribe in Congo he belonged to.

Ever since my arrival in America, I noticed, I did not fancy meeting anyone from back home. America was meant to be a fresh start for me. Congo was home, but there were too many bitter memories in Congo.

In many parts in Africa, one can easily recognize the tribe a person belongs to simply by outward physical appearance. Many blame the colonizers for this. The colonial powers may not have invented the categories such as Hutu or Tutsi, but their actions in many ways intensified the stereotyping. To them, categorizing different tribes according to their outward appearance simply made their administrative governance over the people easier. They did it to divide the population and keep it subjugated.

Over the years, the people progressively began to define themselves according to these European labels. Tutsis were almost always associated with physical attributes such as being tall, stately, and thin, with small noses, while the Bantus were purportedly short and thick-set with large foreheads, wide noses, and enormous lips.

Because there was no appropriate way of asking Ian what his guest looked like, I asked him where specifically he came from.

"I'm not sure which part of Congo he comes from, but you can ask him when you meet him," Ian replied.

"Do you know what language he speaks?" I pressed on.

"Ah, yes! Swahili. He converses in Swahili with the refugees he ministers to."

"Oh, okay, he must be from my mother's town in Kisangani. Her people mostly converse in Swahili too." I quickly realized that I might have sounded relieved, but then I don't think Ian picked up on it.

"Oh, great! You already have something in common."

The evening came and we were still cooking when someone knocked on the door. At the entryway was a short, thickset man wearing a smart but casual shirt. It was our Congolese guest along with his wife and his brother. As soon as we saw each other, we knew that we were from "the other tribe." There was an awkward moment of silence before we greeted one another. His name was Rev. Amahoro. That's a typical Banyamulenge name, I thought to myself. I quickly introduced myself then excused myself and said that I would join them after I was done cooking.

Meanwhile Rev. Amahoro and his family settled in the living room with Ian. I joined them as soon as I finished cooking. I was rather pleased that the memorable smells of Maman's special dish filled the air. The smell took me back home and reminded me of the comforts of tasting Maman's delicious dishes. As I settled in on the couch, I realized that they were discussing the plight of the pygmies of Africa.

"The Bantu governments have forced them to stop living in the rain forests. Where else can they go? The forests are their culture's bedrock. As a Congolese I feel a duty to be a voice for them as I fear their unique traditional way might be gone forever." Rev. Amahoro sounded very passionate about his work and I couldn't help but share my two cents about the topic.

I had never imagined I would share a meal with a Banyamulenge family. I felt like a brand-new person, liberated from bitterness and prejudice toward people of other tribes.

"Yes, that's true," I heard myself say. "They are unique. I mean how many civilizations in the world can actually claim existence for more than a millennium?"

"Whoa! an entire millennium? That is definitely something," Ian exclaimed, in wide-eyed wonder.

That conversation broke the ice for us that day. The rest of the night progressed well. We spoke at great length about our lives, and in that moment, I felt as if I was back in Congo as I listened to the colorful tales he shared of the years he spent there. An instant connection is forged when you meet someone who shares your history, memories, or experiences. Especially, memories made on home soil. The memories may not always be sweet, but they still make up a big part of your life, and that brings comfort, each time.

I told Rev. Mutambo that I was from the Bantu tribe; he then confirmed my initial guess. I had never imagined I would share a meal with a Banyamulenge family. I felt like a brand-new person, liberated from bitterness and prejudice toward people of other tribes. It was as if this get-together had brought springtime to my soul. I told them how I felt, how this meeting was truly a God-sent intervention for me. My testimony then led to a conversation about reconciliation.

"If only people could understand that reconciliation is not necessarily something that we do for others, it's something that we do for ourselves. It's something we do to liberate our soul."

I agreed.

"Trésor, I am feeling a strong conviction at this moment that you will be able to bring a message of hope and reconciliation to my people," Rev. Amahoro suddenly said.

"Me? How do you know that I would be able to do so?" I was shocked at the direction this conversation was going.

"Because you understand what they've been through. You understand the pain and loss they have experienced, and you know how sweet the taste of reconciliation can be. There is a reason that God has brought you through these experiences. You must share it with the people."

This is serious, I thought. I felt the palms of my hands getting wet and clammy. The thought of speaking on a public sphere caused me anxiety. How am I supposed to get through with this?

"There's a conference taking place this coming April in Indianapolis. We're expecting about 300 participants. Most of them are Banyamulenge. Your story would tie in with our Easter theme on reconciliation. The people need to hear this, Trésor..."

His voice started echoing off into the distance. I wasn't listening anymore, just watching his mouth move as I imagined 300 people looking straight at me. *How do I tell him I hate talking about my past to even one person, let alone more than 300? I'm not doing this*, I thought.

"So, Trésor? What do you think?" He was looking directly at me.

Everyone was looking at me.

Then it just happened, the word came out like vomit. I had no control over it. I just spat it out. "Yes," I said. I couldn't believe my ears. I had just agreed to tell a crowd of 300 I no longer hate them anymore.

I was shaken by my willingness to speak at the conference, and

I spent many restless nights picturing the worst. I thought about what the extremists from both sides would think if there were videos shared online. I knew the pastor was willing to welcome me, but I wasn't sure if his community would do the same.

How could I not speak about my past? It was my past that had brought me here; it's what made me who I am.

I had only two months to prepare before this conference. I prayed fervently for courage. God had given me something to say, He had put me in a "privileged" position to have experienced the torments of a war, and He had delivered me from the chains of unforgiveness.

How could I possibly not share this with others? How could I not speak about my past? It was my past that had brought me here; it's what made me who I am.

As the weeks passed, I was more and more convinced that this message of reconciliation was more for me than for them. It was something I had to go through, just another event that was part of the journey to my destiny.

As I traveled to Indianapolis that April, I felt assured that something big was about to happen. I knew what I was about to say, but I still didn't quite have a plan as to how I was going to deliver the message. Ian and Katy came to the conference with me. I was so relieved to have Ian calm my nerves with his sense of humor, and Katy, well, she was always a pleasure to have as company.

The conference was not one of the typical conferences I was used to attending in Bible college. I had never before been to a conference with so many Africans in attendance. Several speakers were due to speak that day, and some were taking longer than the time allotted. My turn to speak kept being delayed. I wondered if the organizers were hesitant to bring someone from the "other tribe" on stage. Almost two hours after my original slot to speak was scheduled, it was finally my turn to take the stage. Over the past few days, I had had a strong inclination to speak on something symbolic. I know how symbolic African culture can be, and I hoped doing something symbolic might strike a chord for some of them.

Before going on stage, I asked one of the organizers for a towel and a bowl of water. He took one good look at me, then looked away and just walked off. He clearly ignored my request, after judging me by my outward appearance. A tiny gesture, comical in retrospect, but it did cause me some pain at the time. So, I asked Ian if he could help me find a bowl of water and a towel, and he did.

> You may be wounded, you may be poor, you may have lost your home and your family, but there is always a way to still have hope, and that is through forgiveness.

My walk to the stage felt like a long journey. My feet were heavy, and my heart beat as if it would pound out of my chest. I took the microphone and began to share my heart with the three hundred people in attendance that day about the hurt and the pain I had felt all my life due to the war in Congo. The words were just flowing out of my mouth, I don't know how, but they did and, at least to me, every word I spoke mirrored my own mind and heart. The more I spoke, the more indignant I became.

"For most of my life, I believed that I had the right to hate, and for most of your lives, the shape of my face and the accent I speak with has probably made you hate me without knowing me." The sanctuary fell into a heavy silence. I told them that this was our opportunity to break the chains of bitterness, hatred, and tribalism. "You may be wounded, you may be poor, you may have lost your home and your family, but there is always a way to still have hope, and that is through forgiveness."

I asked Ian to bring the bowl of water as I announced that I was going to wash their pastor's feet. I asked the Lord to forgive me for the years I did not love like he loved me and proceeded to wash Rev. Amaharo's feet.

I heard someone yell, "Hatred, be gone!"

Another voice called out, "Division, be gone!"

Yet another said, "Tribalism, be gone!"

I lifted my head and saw that people had started gathering around the stage. Some were praying along with me, some were taking pictures. Warm tears started rolling down my cheeks. They were tears of joy, for my heart felt light as if it was liberated from a heavy burden. I realized that there were people around me that were crying, as well.

That day and that incident made me realize how powerful the act of forgiveness can be. The churning and clenching feeling in my stomach that I had before I walked on stage had miraculously stopped. Even amid loud applause and cries, a sense of calmness fell over the entire conference room, as if everyone in the room had been set free into an euphoric abyss.

As I turned to leave the stage, I felt the translator on stage with me put his arms around me. It was the warmest hug I had felt in a long time, a comforting and assuring hug such as you would receive from a dear family member. I would have never expected a hug from someone from the "other tribe" to bring me so much comfort and assurance. I took a couple more steps forward and someone else put their arms around me.

"Forgiveness is unlocking a door that you believe would set someone else free, only to realize that you were the actual prisoner behind that door in the first place. Forgive your perpetrators, and that will be the greatest gift you can give yourself." With that, I ended my session that day with a verse taken from the book of Ephesians 4:31-32.

"Get rid of all bitterness, rage and anger, brawling and slander, along with every form of malice. Be kind and compassionate to one another, forgiving each other, just as in Christ God forgave you."

CHAPTER 6

Yet here I am, despite it all

War is merciless, and the wounds from a war are not confined to the battlefield. Even after the carnage has ended, the survivors still carry the wounds. These wounds will turn into visible scars, but the emotional trauma of a war remains largely hidden from view. Long after the sound of gunshots and shelling have ceased, the war still carries on silently in the survivor's mind.

One quiet afternoon between classes I was sitting on the porch at Williamson Hall. It was a normal day, with few people around, and the weather was moderately chilly. As I gazed into the distance, I suddenly heard a loud bang, like a hammer striking on metal. In an instant I recognized the all-too-familiar sound. Gunshots! My heart started pounding in my chest, and my instincts told me to run, hide, and take cover. I frantically looked around me but saw that people were going about their business as usual. Could they not hear the shots, too? I quickly realized that these sounds were going off in my head. They sounded so real! I was sweating profusely in the chilly weather, and my hands were trembling.

"Are you okay? Mister?" I heard a deep voice call out to me.

I blankly gazed on an unknown face and slowly panned down his figure from top to toe. "Are you okay?" He asked again, this time much more calmly.

"Yeah, I'm okay. I'm just going to get some air. I should feel better," I replied, and stood up and walked away.

This wasn't the first time. I had frequently experienced similar moments where I felt the world was too loud and was closing in on me, causing a sudden rush of panic. I couldn't quite figure out what was wrong. All I knew was that I felt scared, far more than I'd ever felt in Congo.

The panic attacks began getting worse after a catastrophic tornado struck Joplin in 2011. The tornado was one of the deadliest tornadoes to strike the United States in fifty years. News outlets and weather experts called it the EF-5 tornado. Whatever its name was, it destroyed everything that came in its way, pummeling brick and mortar, land and life; ultimately it split the southern Missouri city in half.

The loss and grief the city was grappling with was an all-too-familiar feeling. The memories came rushing back and hit me like a ton of bricks. The disaster had taken an emotional toll on me, and I felt as if my safe and secure haven in America was bleeding and in despair; it was no different in comparison to the situation back home in Congo. I slept very little at night, constantly awakened by nightmares. I prayed that the Lord would take away the horrors and give me rest. Sure enough, the Lord had already begun his work on healing my emotions in a way only He could do.

> I felt as if my safe and secure haven in America was bleeding and in despair; it was no different in comparison to the situation back home in Congo.

□ □ □

During my last semester at Ozark I attended the American Association of Christian Counselors Conference. The road trip to Dallas remains one of my all-time favorite memories of America. I was privileged to travel in the company of two of my favorite lecturers at Ozark, Peter Buckland and Gary Zustiak. While walking through the various booths at the exhibition hall, I met Cathy Thorpe, a therapist from Washington State.

Looking back now, I surmise that my encounter with Cathy was not by chance, but by a divine interruption in both our lives. Cathy explained to me how she was trained in using a technique called the healing timeline to help people overcome trauma they had faced at any given point in their lives. She told me that could help alleviate the panic attacks I had been dealing with. We exchanged contact details and kept in touch. Three months after the conference, I flew to Seattle to meet with Cathy. She diligently worked through the timeline therapy that slowly but surely helped change my life. I gradually came to terms with my old wounds and the grief I had bottled up for years. It took me a few weeks to realize that I had had no recent panic attacks.

I wondered how many others walked the streets of Congo hearing gunshots in the midst of pin-drop silence.

Cathy taught me to be grateful despite my experiences. Be grateful that my family had survived, grateful that my home was intact, but, most of all, grateful that I had an opportunity to share my story with others who were also battling inner trauma.

It was the first time in weeks that I came close to being able to sit still. All my fears about the constant, shifting sands that had begun to take form in my life were miraculously suspended. I knew that God's mighty hand was at work, and I felt a renewed passion and conviction to work with others suffering with post-traumatic stress disorders.

I wondered how many others walked the streets of Congo hearing gunshots in the midst of pin-drop silence. I thought of those who went to sleep at night with tears covering their faces and fear crowding their minds. I knew I had to do something.

◻   ◻   ◻

One year later, I met Sheila. Our first encounter was special, and I knew right away that we were going to be good friends. She was a petite, middle-aged woman with prominent blue eyes and shoulder length brown hair. Sheila had a persona that made her a person of the world. She exuded so much warmth and friendliness that very much suited her profession as a medical practitioner. She told me that she wanted to study the mental well-being of those recovering from war-torn circumstances.

As we sat over a sumptuous Thai meal, Sheila explained her interest in Congo. "I became enthralled with the colorful Congolese culture and decided to make it the subject of my study. I know that there are many unseen wounds that hide behind the beautiful smiles of the people and I want to personally hear their stories." A certain expression of sheer determination crossed her face as she spoke. I knew once again that my meeting with Sheila was not by chance but part of God's plan to make my return to Congo a purposeful one.

Sheila asked me if I could help connect her to the right people in Congo.

I remembered my dear Uncle Gaston who was also a medical practitioner living in Kinshasa. I almost jumped with delight at her request. "I would be glad to show you my home."

We quickly began planning and preparing for our trip to Congo. Planning and preparing was an adventure in itself. My uncle Gaston agreed to introduce us to the right people to make interviews and visits for Sheila's study as informative as possible. Certain academic requirements had to be met for the trip to be officially approved, and we labored to tie up all the loose ends on our part.

Whenever I felt overwhelmed by the preparation before us, I would calm myself by thinking of fond memories from back home. I closed my eyes and pictured Maman in her tiny garden, walking around her potted plants, inspecting the leaves, her plain cotton dress fluttering in the breeze. Warm biscuits and the scent of lavender was what I thought Maman smelled like when she enveloped me with her hugs. I could not wait to go home.

After weeks of preparation, we were finally ready to embark. Sheila left first, accompanied by her son Seth, who also had a keen interest in learning about the subject that his mother was very passionate about. "She would talk about it for hours! I must see what Congo is like!" I was delighted to have Seth share the experience with us.

There was so much positive build-up leading up to the trip, I thought nothing could go wrong. Indeed, all was going well, until the moment I missed my flight from Kansas City on the day of my intended departure.

We had not even started the trip, and I was already facing a roadblock. I was disappointed about missing my flight but kept my spirits up and told myself that everything happens for a purpose. Perhaps there is some reason why I missed the flight.

Sure enough, I met some very interesting people on my way to Congo through Brussels. Going through the airport in Brussels often makes me feel as if I am already in Congo. The airport setup is similar, and a lot of Congolese work there. While waiting at the boarding gate, I tried my best to entertain myself. Search for free Wi-Fi connections, read a book, check fifty times to see if I am at the right gate, and occasionally glance around to people-watch.

Then I noticed the woman in front of me had accidentally dropped her boarding pass. I called out to her and reached for the boarding pass on the floor. She profusely thanked me after I handed over the pass to her. She was accompanied by a man who looked similar in age to her. They were probably in their mid-30s, both wearing the same shade of jeans, carrying matching luggage. A certain aura surrounded them, one that was hard to miss, excitement or anticipation of some sort. We asked each other where we were headed and let out a short laugh when we realized we were all headed to Congo. The couple introduced themselves; they were from Kentucky.

"We're going to Congo to adopt a baby," the wife told me enthusiastically.

She had a wide smile and a glimmer in the corners of her eyes as she spoke. I felt so happy for them and at the same time glad to know that there was a system in place that enabled children to find good homes with good families to grow up with. We spoke at length about the adoption process before realizing that it was already time to board the flight. We exchanged farewells, and I wished them the best as they began their life as a new family.

As I walked into the aircraft I realized how exhausted I was and hoped to have a row to myself to catch up on some much-needed rest. I settled in my seat, but no one came to occupy the seats on either side. Another answered prayer, I thought to myself, and closed my eyes. The plane took off, but as soon as the seatbelt signs were off, I heard some noise in the back. It sounded like loud, angry voices. I ignored the noise and tried to find a comfortable spot in my row.

My mind was racing. I was mentally ticking off my list of things to do as soon as I arrived in Kinshasa. There's so much to do, I thought, and slowly closed my eyes again. Then I heard some rummaging in the seat next to me and opened my eyes to see an older woman of African descent placing her bag on the floor by my legs.

"Do you mind if I take this seat?" Her voice sounded feeble as if she was panting.

I nodded with a small smile.

"The man seated next to me was very drunk, he started vomiting all over."

"Oh, so that's what the commotion was all about," I replied, slightly disappointed I had lost my space. "Hope you're okay, though?"

She looked sluggardly and spiritless as if something was bothering her. "Yeah, I'm fine. Thanks," she replied with a smile.

In the seat in front of us were two men. They were in a deep discussion about Congolese children and witchcraft, a growing problem in Congo. I felt very strongly about the subject, so I turned off my media screen and paid attention to their conversation.

"There's a widespread belief, especially in the southern parts of Congo, that children can carry powerful powers akin to sorcerers. If a relative or neighbor was killed by a disease for instance, fingers are pointed at innocent children. Even parents are quick to accuse their children who wet their beds or who suffer from symptoms of epilepsy as witches."

I was all too familiar with this and could not resist the urge to join in on their conversation. I leaned over their seats and introduced myself and shared how a distant relative of mine from my father's province in Bukavu was accused of witchcraft and shunned by his family as a result. He was only a child.

"These persecutions seem to be encouraged by mushrooming cults in the south," one man chimed in. He introduced himself as a neurosurgeon working on his doctorate in Belgium. He was coming back to serve the country as one out of only four neurosurgeons in Congo.

The other man was a Congolese church leader. Christianity in Congo is professed by a majority of the population, so meeting a fellow Congolese Christian was quite common. I told them that I was a student at a Bible college in America and that I was headed home to Congo to participate in a study project on trauma.

"Interesting," the neurosurgeon remarked. "The Congolese society is a very traumatized society. It's good to know that there are efforts being made to correct this condition."

The Congolese society is a very traumatized society.

As we got deeper in our conversation, the lady sitting next to me interrupted and told us that she had been battling sleep issues for several years. She confessed that when it was quiet, she heard gunshots. She had recurring nightmares and moments when she thought she was experiencing symptoms of a heart attack, as if she was about to die.

I shared my story of recovery from PTSD with her and told her that I'd like to pray for her. As I was praying for her I heard her sobbing; she was clearly dealing with a heavy burden. The horrors of the war had crippled her with anxiety, yet on the surface she was trying to remain strong. That's when I realized that my journey had already begun right there, right at that moment, in the plane to Kinshasa. God was already using me to bring healing to the lives of my fellow people whose emotions and mental well-being had been damaged. God had gone before me, and this moment was a clear indication.

Before we left the plane, I gave her the contact details of a mental health facility in Kinshasa. "Therapy and prayer will help get you through this," I told her.

She thanked me, and I noticed a different aura about her. It was the look of someone who had finally reached a state of peace and acceptance.

CHAPTER 7

Faith can move mountains

Once I landed in Kinshasa, there was no time to rest. I had friends waiting for me, and new adventures were about to begin. Though exhausted by almost two days of intense travel, I was eager to see my father at the airport to receive me. Instead, I saw my cousin at the receiving gate but was equally excited to see him after so long. Fewer people were at the airport this time, and there was some kind of order in the airport for once. Nevertheless, the airport was still noisy. I think everyone tries to be loud here.

My heart leaped with joy as we came out of the terminal when I saw the red soil in the distance that distinctly meant I was back home in Africa. My sisters were waiting for me in the car, and as soon as I saw them, I couldn't help but think about my mother's cooking and how I would be sleeping on my own bed tonight.

Each day, tens of thousands of people—business owners, students, workers and people looking for work—walk along the new road because they can't afford to ride in anything that uses it.

As we left the airport to make our way back to my house, I stared out the window, deep in thought. The sun was shining; it was a hot and humid day, the air still. I began noticing the tiniest of details around me. Perhaps the exposure that I had gained while abroad enabled me to perceive my surroundings differently. I noticed that the road from the airport to downtown perfectly encapsulates the history and challenges facing Kinshasa today.

The brand new four-lane highway, built with inter-national funds, is regarded as one of the best infrastructures in the country. With smooth, black asphalt, shiny white lines and deep concrete ditches to catch the tropical downpours, the road is meant to improve the city's desperately poor transportation infrastructure. And it does. But along the edges, I observed that, so little had changed.

Kinshasa is the urban pulse of Congo, yet at the same time a boulevard of broken dreams. Each day, tens of thousands of people—business owners, students, workers and people looking for work—walk along the new road because they can't afford to ride in anything that uses it.

Spreading out across the banks of the Congo River and foothills of Congo sits Kinshasa. In the few years since I left, it had grown so big, so wide and so busy. I was still enthralled by the small vendors on the streets selling sweets, water, beer, mobile-phone credit, and small bundles of fish or cassava loaves wrapped in banana leaves.

The familiar mounds of litter collected in the eddies of the traffic jams, coated in layers of dust from the dirt side roads, along with ash and soot from small piles of burning garbage. So much was going on. Kinshasa never failed to galvanize as a town that courses with energy, as though the scorching sun above it is breathing down on everyone's neck.

After a day's rest and quality family time, I was ready to embark on the real reason for my return to Congo. Sheila and Seth were waiting for me at a mental health facility that Uncle Gaston had arranged for us to visit. We had a few mental health facilities on our list, but the Telema Mental Health Center (TMHC) was first on our schedule.

Without a doubt, the need for mental health facilities in Congo is high, yet its provision remains limited. Less than one percent of the government's health budget goes toward this area of healthcare. This was evident as soon as I saw the mediocre state of the mental health clinic we visited.

We were met at the entryway of the clinic by a Spanish nurse who introduced herself as Sister Angele. She stood at the entranceway and coldly interrogated us on the purpose of our visit.

"Why do you want to conduct a study here?" she asked with a straight face. "Where are you all from?"

I explained in detail that our visit was part of a research study on how the Congolese are dealing with trauma from the war. Sheila pulled out an official letter, which in Congo is known as an *orde du mission*. She seemed more convinced thereafter and stepped aside to let us in to the facility.

Many victims, when faced with symptoms of mental disorders are ostracized and banished by their loved ones due to a belief that witchcraft and sorcery might be the reason behind their symptoms.

Sister Angele's demeanor was understandable, consider-ing the prevailing social stigma associated with mental health problems. She deeply cared for and was protective of those at the clinic. Many victims, when faced with symptoms of mental disorders are ostracized and banished by their loved ones due to a belief that witchcraft and sorcery might be the reason behind their symptoms.

"If only we had more support from the governmental bodies, that would be good. But the budget allocated to us is tiny and our challenges are huge. Yet God has always made a way and provided for us in our times of need," she explained with a smile.

God is in the big things, but He is also very much in the small little things too. When we trust him in the small things, he will entrust us with the bigger things.

We would go on to make many more visits to TMHC, and Sister Angele over time became a personal friend and partner. Her valuable insights and wisdom on treating people with trauma helped Sheila's research immensely. We would see how determined she was to improve the outlook for her mental health patients.

Women like Sister Angele who display immense faith in times of uncertainty inspire me tremendously. Sister Angele reminds me of my mother. Maman had always been a woman of faith. As a young boy, she frequently shared anecdotes of miracles God had bestowed upon our family in our times of need. "God is in the big things, but He is also very much in the small little things too. When we trust him in the small things, he will entrust us with the bigger things," she constantly reminded us.

One of my favorite stories from Maman was the story of my birth. Maman has repeated this story numerous times, and I never get tired of hearing it. Every time I hear the story, I feel the same wonder and hope swelling inside me as I did upon hearing it for the very first time.

I was born during a difficult time for my parents. They lacked the money to pay the hospital bill, nor could they afford baby clothes. On the grounds that my parents could not afford to pay, my mother and I were detained in the hospital till we found the means to settle the pending bill.

This was 1983, thirty-six years ago. Unfortunately, this predicament is still a reality for many new Congolese mothers. At the hospital, these mothers are held behind large gates, carrying their infants in their arms. Some are even detained for several months because they are unable to settle the costs of their deliveries.

Maman would go on to tell us that despite having to face the unknown, despite being unable to provide basic clothing for her newborn, she was certain that God would make a way to provide for her every need. Soon enough, a distant relative came by the hospital. He brought the nicest clothing and even settled the hospital bill for Maman. This man did precisely what Maman had been praying for; it was everything that she had needed.

The man said he had felt a prompting, a still small voice telling him to respond to the prayer Maman was sending his way. Maman said that I was dressed like a little prince the day I left the hospital. For many years thereafter, I thought of this kind man and the voice that spoke to him and wondered if one day I would hear that voice, too, prompting me to help many of those in need in the hospitals of Congo.

I wonder how many others have heard this voice.

Twenty-one years after that first miracle in my life, I found myself in America, working hard at a physical plant in college, trying to make ends meet. Fixing things was assuredly not one of my strengths, but I was a hard worker and slowly I picked up the skill. It helped to have supportive colleagues to show me the ropes around the plant. One colleague was Rick, through whom I developed a strong foundation of good work ethics which still come in useful.

One day, as we were going about our duties at the plant, Rick asked me about Christmastime in Congo. He wanted to know how families in Congo spent their holidays. I explained that Christmas in Congo was more a religious festival than a commercial one. Most people won't have any presents. But whether rich or poor, parents always do their best to provide their children with the best meals they can afford. Food in general, but especially chicken and other meat, becomes very expensive during the Christmas season. Nevertheless, it's a celebration everyone looks forward to. A few days later, Rick handed me an envelope with three hundred dollars.

"Merry Christmas, Trésor!" he said gleefully.

As I received the envelope, a nagging voice in my head kept saying, "It is more blessed to give than to receive." As the day progressed I thought about home, how I would be missing out on Christmas celebrations with my family. Just like that, like a bolt of lightning, I knew what I had to do.

It didn't take long to recognize the voice that had been nagging me, and within minutes I called my mother to ask her if she could organize a visit to the Saint Joseph Hospital in Kinshasa. "I have three hundred dollars. Can you deliver some food to those in the hospital?" I asked her.

Maman was happy to visit the hospital with a small group that consisted of my sisters, Joela, 16, and Rose, 19. With the money, they prepared several packets consisting of a handful of rice to distribute to the patients in need. To many of the patients in the hospital, a handful of rice is a Christmas feast. They celebrated because someone somewhere thought of them in their time of need.

Maman called me after the visit with good news that the money I sent brought joy to many. She reminded me not to underestimate the power of giving, no matter how small. "Even a single grain of rice can tip a scale. A handful of rice, now that can weigh as heavy as a mountain." Those words will stay with me forever.

To many of the patients in the hospital, a handful of rice is a Christmas feast. They celebrated because someone somewhere thought of them in their time of need.

CHAPTER 8

There can be no true freedom, so long as poverty persists

Organizing my first hospital feeding initiative was an exhilarating experience for me. Although I could not be there personally, I felt connected to those that received the tiny packages and celebrated their blessings that day. The realization that a small gesture of giving could bring about such tremendous impact for someone in Congo gave me a sharper purpose than I ever had before.

It felt as if a sudden surge of motivation had engulfed my life, propelling me to work harder, to spread the word and to continue facilitating more feeding initiatives for my people back home.

Meanwhile, in Congo, a small team of young people would get together to purchase basic provisions, pack it into small packages, and distribute it in the hospitals. These young people only consisted of my two younger sisters, Rose, Joelle and some close friends. It was moving to see how dedicated my family and friends were to help make these initiatives happen.

It was moving to see how dedicated my family and friends were to help make these initiatives happen.

I was not the only one going around making conversation about how people were starving in hospitals across Congo, it started becoming a part of their everyday conversation as well.

My friend Grace Mbuthia, one of our pioneer staff members, once told me, "Friends are the family you choose." She was right. I could not have been more grateful for the group of friends I had chosen.

Before leaving the U.S. for my trip back to Congo with Sheila and Seth, I sent an email informing everyone on our team to make all the necessary preparations for another hospital feeding initiative. Then, I announced the good news. This time around I would personally be there to join them together with Sheila and Seth, who would be our guests from the U.S. I was confident that the project was going to be a good learning experience for all of us; and it was, just not quite in a way that I had expected.

It was one of those June days when the sunshine could soak right into your bones, one of the hottest months of the year in Congo. The usual team of volunteers gathered at my parents' house to pack basic provisions, including sugar, milk, soap, and rice. We spent an hour packing these little bags to the brim. I thought about how these packets looked so small and insignificant, yet each small packet—just a handful of food—represented hope the size of a mountain for those at the hospital.

Midway through our preparations, Joelle reminded me to pack envelopes containing cash that we had specially allocated for this visit. The cash envelopes were going to be used to free patients that were detained in the hospital. You see, our visit this time was unlike the other hospital visits the team had been carrying out. This time our feeding initiative would take place in a hospital jail, a concept that has always been tough to explain to my foreign friends.

The collapse of the economy due to the ongoing war had enmeshed the hospitals in Congo in a complex state of crisis. Meager funding meant that hospitals in Congo ran on subpar budgets and lacked basic necessities. Equipment was scarce, waiting rooms and wards dimly lit, and medical personnel lacked proper training and experience.

When a patient has to undergo surgery, the family is responsible for finding the surgical supplies. A supply list—from gloves, to anything else that the doctor may need—is given to the family. They must find everything to facilitate the surgery. In addition, the families must also solicit money as a nominal fee for the surgery to take place.

With every passing moment, the patient's condition deteriorates, and death draws closer. For those who scrape through the process, the final bill must be settled or else the patient is put in the hospital jail. This is where those who have successfully undergone treatment but cannot afford to pay are held until their families find a way to pay the final fee. An average patient's bill is about twenty-five dollars. While that seems small to most of us, it is a fortune for most Congolese, who earn less than a dollar a day.

The final bill must be settled or else the patient is put in the hospital jail.

We only had a budget of two hundred dollars, and I felt anxious, thinking about how we had to select just a few out of the many that needed help. *How am I going to make the choice?* I often wondered.

As we drove to the hospital, we sat in the vehicle, all silent. Each of us knew that the visit would be a difficult one. Having to decide who gets to go home and who has to stay would haunt our consciences, but we had to do what we could with what we had. Sheila then reminded us of a quote by Mother Theresa: "If you can't feed a hundred people, then feed just one." *It is the first step that matters*, I thought as I stared out the window, *the rest will follow. Perhaps someday I will be back with much more to give and won't need to choose.*

After we arrived at the hospital, we met with the hospital's social service officer. He was a large man with a wide face and stern expression. The uniform he was wearing seemed old and a little frayed at the ends.

As we walked toward the jail wards, he painstakingly explained why they had to enforce this system for the patients. "We can't just let people leave if they don't pay," he explained in Lingala. "It is not a good feeling for us working here to see them kept like this, but no one ever comes back to pay their bill a month or two later. If the hospital releases them, it will have to run at a loss and we workers here won't get paid. You see, that's just how a business works."

The situation was hard for both sides, and the only solution seemed to be detaining the patients until their family or a charity could pay some of the charges. Some who could not afford their bills spent up to sixty days at the hospital.

The political and economic collapse of the country over the past three decades had drastically impacted the health care system.

I felt both anger and compassion at the same time. The political and economic collapse of the country over the past three decades had drastically impacted the health care system. The problem the hospital was facing was deeply rooted, tied to the problems of the entire country. The information that the social worker left us prompted us to think deeper than what we saw that day. People who needed help "here and now" didn't have another day to wait.

We were first taken to the pediatric ward. On the way, I noted a few checkpoints, used to control movement; in the hospital it was an incongruous sight. Visitor badges were thoroughly checked. A receipt or a badge was required before leaving an area. So many restrictions were in place to ensure that detained patients did not leave the hospital; I could already feel a churning in the pit of my stomach. The hospital seemed every bit a jail. How was anyone meant to make a full recovery here?

Their eyes spoke more than any words; their silence made more noise than an explosion. They were begging us to free them, and in that moment my heart broke for them.

As we entered the room, the social worker pointed out those in most desperate need. We saw mothers holding their newborns. They lifted their heads and looked into our eyes. Their eyes spoke more than any words; their silence made more noise than an explosion. They were begging us to free them, and in that moment my heart broke for them. I said a prayer for those that we could not help.

Being forced to choose who to help that day was one of the hardest decisions I would make in my life. I finally decided to pay for a set of twins. Sheila chose another patient. We gave them the gift of freedom to go home, but there were still so many others yearning for such a gift.

We were asked to wait in front of the office while the social worker went to pay the bills. Very quickly there were chairs placed outside to accommodate us. The word had gotten out that we were there paying bills. Suddenly there were random women that brought their chairs to sit with us. They wanted us to hear their stories and those of their children in hopes that we would help pay their bills too.

Each one of these women had a child; each one genuinely needed help. We were their only hope for a chance to return home, and we had exhausted all our resources. No money remained to help these ladies, and I felt utterly powerless. We listened to their stories and told them we had no more money.

Soon thereafter, the social worker came back. We were relieved to see him. He introduced us to the families that had been freed from the hospital jail. Their faces radiated joy as they thanked us for enabling them to return home to their loved ones.

Just as we were leaving, a woman grabbed Sheila's hand. She wore a look of desperation on her face as she explained that she needed seven dollars to buy supplies for a surgery for her child. We knew the visit to the hospital would take an emotional toll on us, but hearing how seven dollars could save a child's life hit us harder than we ever thought it could. We emptied our pockets of whatever spare change we had and managed to accumulate a little over seven dollars. What's meant to be will always find a way. I guess it was meant to be for that little child to get his surgery fee supplied that day.

We would never be the same again after that visit. Though our efforts only amounted to a tiny drop in the ocean, at the same time we had to remind ourselves that if that tiny drop was not there, the ocean would be missing something.

CHAPTER 9

Listen to your heart, it knows

My return to Congo had thus far taught me that I am just a small creature in a large landscape. Each person I had met and each place I visited had a great story of its own, and each story had made me a modest person. I realized what a tiny place I occupied in the grand scheme of things. Yet the experiences I had collected along the way were enormous, and I yearned to share these experiences with others.

I knew that both Sheila and Seth felt the same way. Their experiences had likewise transformed their perspectives. And these experiences were meant to be shared, not kept. We were about to get our chance to share our stories with those who needed to hear it in a small town called Menkao.

Uncle Gaston had told us that a special polio vaccination day was coming up and that health institutions across the country had set a target to eradicate the disease within a brief span of time. Uncle asked if we would be willing to volunteer on this day. Our group agreed, of course. It sounded like a significant cause, and we wanted to lend a hand in any way possible.

Menkao is a rural city located outside of Kinshasa but still within the province itself. The road out of Kinshasa City took us past rolling green hills that hung menacingly over the province. There were abundant greeneries to feast our eyes on and endless banana plants along the roads. I rolled the window down and took a deep breath to smell the freshness of the rural air. A woman was walking by the side of the road with a bucket of water on her head. It was reassuring to know that mother nature continues to have a significant stake in Kinshasa because it sure did not seem so in the usual hustle and bustle of the city center.

We reached the medical center that was to serve as the base for the vaccinations and were told it was the only medical facility within a fifteen-kilometer radius. As we were given a tour of the center, I noticed posters on the walls illustrating the basics of dealing with leprosy. The posters left me stunned—I was under the impression that leprosy was a disease consigned to Biblical times.

"There are people still living with leprosy today? And right here in Congo?" I asked the male nurse that was showing us around.

"Yes," he replied solemnly. "We still receive cases of people living with leprosy from around the area. Many people still ostracize them and believe they are cursed, and because of the lack of support and ignorance, eradicating the disease is still a challenge," he explained, as I studied the posters and understood that it is in fact a curable disease, thanks to modern science and technology.

After the tour, we were briefed on our tasks and began the rounds. It was a rather simple process. The vaccination was to be given to young children under five years old by consuming the liquid medication orally. We were also briefed on facts and statistics on polio incidents in Congo. The World Health Organization recommends that every child be given the necessary vaccinations for polio as part of a campaign to ensure a polio-free world for future generations.

As volunteers, our sole aim was to approach people on the street or in their homes to reach every last child in the village. Parents in homes cooperated far better than the ones we met on the streets. On one street, they asked one of us to consume the vaccine first to prove it was not some kind of poison.

It was painful to watch my fellow people of the same soil trust Sheila and Seth more than they trusted the rest of us.

I realized that the people were still harboring old wounds and old fears that people of their own kind could kill their loved ones. That fear was so deeply ingrained. It was painful to watch my fellow people of the same soil trust Sheila and Seth more than they trusted the rest of us.

I volunteered to drink the vaccine to prove to the

local villagers that the drops would in no way harm them, just help them. Gradually word spread, and people started bringing their children to us. I guess small towns are very much like glass houses, everyone can see what you're doing and that worked to our benefit.

While we were walking, I noticed several mud houses, but one house stood out. This house was made of wood and had a roof made of tin and corrugated iron. Someone had planted flowers in pots neatly arranged outside the front porch of the house. Beige cotton curtains hung in the windows.

We walked toward the house and heard a beautiful sound of traditional drums gradually getting louder the closer we walked. The smell of grilled fish and ugali, a stiff porridge made from maize meal, filled our senses and reminded me that I was hungry.

"That's a local church and it's probably praise and worship time right now," Uncle Gaston explained.

"Their lunch smells delicious. What is that?" Sheila asked.

"Grilled fish. It's a specialty in this area. They catch it fresh from the river. We must try some of the fish from the local marketplace."

Uncle Gaston had truly outdone himself as our host. To top it all, it was Sheila's birthday. What better way to spend her birthday than savoring local delicacies? We were all thrilled to be able to share the day with her. Before we left, Uncle Gaston mentioned that some of the world's rarest fish could be found in the marketplace. We could hardly sit still, we had to be there already.

We drove through more hills and green pastures on our way to the marketplace. As we reached the riverbanks, I remembered how fond I was of the river. There's something magical about it. Every time I set my eyes on it, I could feel it breathing almost as if it was alive. More than anything else, this majestic river was the heartbeat of Congo. Over hundreds and thousands of years, the river has rushed down from the hills, hauling the town's dirt, filling the seas, giving us fish and making trees grow. The river was what made Congo Congo, and it would always be that way.

Clad in our volunteer t-shirts, we were ready to discover the riverside marketplace. While basking in the sights and smells, we occasionally tasted, too. At one point, when we stopped at one of the stalls, I spied from the corner of my eye that my uncle looked somewhat nervous and uncomfortable. I tried to figure out what it was that could have possibly changed his mood, just then I noticed a man walking swiftly toward us. It took just a brief moment before it struck me that our volunteer t-shirts and the presence of foreigners in those t-shirts could carry a wrong message, especially with certain government authorities.

"I am impressed that you are even vaccinating fishes nowadays!" the man sarcastically exclaimed. Uncle Gaston tried to explain why we were there, who we were and what we were doing. Then the man burst into a light giggle. "I was just teasing! It's always good to see volunteers that are willing to lend a helping hand to change the state of health affairs in Congo."

Uncle Gaston looked so relieved. I saw some color return to his suddenly pale face. The man introduced himself as a medical officer, which explained his interest in our work. In return, we introduced ourselves in Lingala, then introduced Sheila, noting that she was a nurse and university professor.

He wanted more details about our vaccination initiative and asked a few questions about Sheila before he wished us a beautiful Sunday and excused himself. We enjoyed the rest of the day at the marketplace and came back to Kinshasa shortly after nightfall. Once again, I basked in the sights on our drive back home. It felt serene to watch nighttime drawing down like a blind by the riverside.

The mountains formed a black wall against the fading pink of the sky as the sun slowly set. Far away, at the foot of the hills, one by one, sprinkles of yellow lights appeared. There were people there, some cooking dinner, some putting their children to bed, most of them settling in for the night.

The next day Uncle Gaston called to inform me that the man we met was actually a national vaccination supervisor for the Ministry of Health. The man had gone on to share his encounter with Sheila, the university professor and medical officer from America, with his colleagues. As a result, the president of the Congolese Nurses Association got in touch with Uncle Gaston, requesting a meeting at his office with the American professor.

When Uncle Gaston told me, I hesitated, as we were hard-pressed for time and had several other commitments over the last few days before making our way back to America. Yet I had a hunch that the meeting could be beneficial for Sheila's research. She might be able to collect some additional data from the nurses association, I thought, so we agreed to meet.

We were told that the primary purpose of our meeting would be for the leaders at the nurses association to draw from Sheila's experiences about practicing nursing in America. But when Sheila said that she was a member of The American Board of Nurses, our meeting took a turn in a different direction altogether.

Congo's health service is currently facing a dire shortage of nurses. Nurses are overworked and underpaid, so many are leaving to pursue better opportunities overseas. Nurses had been lobbying tirelessly to pass a law in parliament that would allow them to set up a board of nurses in Congo. This board would be able to uphold the basic rights of nurses and push for reforms to increase wages for nurses across the country.

It was going to be a momentous meeting; I would serve as translator. Translating medical English would be challenging, and it made me nervous because I did not want to mistranslate any important points that Sheila would share. Nevertheless, a sense of unabated eagerness flowed out of me. I had an inclination that something consequential would come of this.

The meeting was held at the Ngaliema Hospital, one of the

reference hospitals in Kinshasa. When we arrived, we found groups of people already seated in the hall, ready for the session to start. More and more people were walking in; soon a large crowd was present. The meeting was obviously a pivotal one, and many people were eagerly waiting to pick Sheila's brain.

Sheila opened her session by sharing her testimony about her choosing the nursing profession by way of answering to a higher calling in her life. With great passion, Sheila shared how God called her to this vocation of helping people. I studied the audience in between translating and noted the intense look of focus visible on their faces as she spoke about how she met the Lord and decided to serve God through her profession as a nurse.

"Your profession is not what brings home your weekly or your monthly paychecks. Your profession is what you are put on earth to do. You should work with such passion and intensity that you make your passion your paycheck and that will fulfill you forever."

A sense of eagerness was spewing out of me. I had an inclination that something consequential would come of this.

Sheila's words of wisdom that day were profound, almost as if an anointed force was speaking on her behalf. I felt so proud watching and hearing her inspire the medical officers present. Then came the technical aspect of Sheila's talk. She gave a rundown on the history behind the formation of the American Board of Nurses and its role in the nursing community. She gave some tips about how the medical officers can go about setting up their own board of nurses.

Your profession is not what brings home your weekly or your monthly paychecks. Your profession is what you are put on earth to do.

People were captivated by all she said, but mostly they were touched by her testimony and her personal story. There were a few questions at the end, but after an hour and a half, the session ended.

Those ninety minutes were all it took for God to work His way to encourage the medical officers and decision makers present that day. The law was finally passed in 2016 and an official government-endorsed board of nurses was established. The president of the nurses association got in touch with me, asking me to thank Mama Sheila for inspiring the health officials through her story and for being part of their victory. The nursing community in Congo never forgot her.

Looking back, I now believe that following your intuition—even if it defies logic or practicality—can be a game-changer. In this case, had I done the practical thing to decline the meeting invitation and keep to our schedule, we would not have come across a golden opportunity.

That strong inclination within me could not have been clearer; I was so glad that I followed it. That ninety-minute meeting opened the door to a monumental partnership that we enjoy with the Ministry of Health of Congo up to this day.

CHAPTER 10

Your light will rise
in the darkness,
and your night will
become like the
noonday

Upon my return to America, I was hounded with assignments and research to finish the final leg of my studies at Evangel Bible School. At the same time, I was having trouble catching a good night's rest. Every night I would think about how each person that I had met on my recent trip back home had made an appearance in my life for a distinct reason. I started to struggle with an intense feeling of guilt.

Out of the millions of babies born in Congo, I was born into the lottery of life with a winning ticket—a loving family, a chance to pursue a good education and good health. But what had I done to deserve any of it? Why was I born into those blessings when so many others were born into suffering? Why was I here in a booming and safe city when my fellow countrymen and -women were born in villages without electricity, food or water?

> I strongly felt the time had come for me to start up a nonprofit of some kind that could serve the people back home.

I was reluctant to admit it, but I felt that I owed something to my people. I spent nights tossing in my bed till I realized that I was placed in a position of privilege to pass on the gifts that I had received. Each person that I had met was placed in my life to inspire and guide me in my journey to provide greater opportunities for others. I was experiencing a major emotional swing, and I strongly felt the time had come for me to start up a nonprofit of some kind that could serve the people back home.

One evening, I decided to attend a faith forum. The focus of the forum that day was on learning how to defend your faith. We were halfway through, and I was having a hard time concentrating. I dozed off. There had been a lot of sleepless nights preparing for my thesis, and it was so hard to keep my eyes open.

I woke suddenly to see that the forum was already
at the question-and-answer session. Feeling slightly
embarrassed to have missed the end; I opened my
Bible and randomly flipped pages. Just like that, a
verse leaped off one of the pages at me. The verse was
from **Isaiah 58:10**: *"And if you spend yourselves in behalf
of the hungry and satisfy the needs of the oppressed, then
your light will rise in the darkness and your night will
become like the noonday."*

Reading that verse over and over again made me
once again contemplate my desire to start something
bigger than myself. Start something that could move
others as well. People sometimes think that big ideas
suddenly appear on their own, but mine wasn't like
that.

My big idea was actually the product of many small
intersecting moments and realizations that propelled
me towards a breakthrough. I thought about the light
that I could bring in times of darkness and suddenly a
name shot across my mind.

Mwangaza, which means "shining light" in
Swahili.

> I thought about
> the light that I
> could bring in
> times of darkness
> and suddenly a
> name shot across
> my mind.

I felt as if a bolt of lightning went right
through me. Light is one of the most universal
and fundamental symbols. Light is the source
of goodness. In the Bible light is defined as
life and the only way to receive "life" is to be known of
the light through God and his son, Jesus.

My mind surged with ideas, and my fists clenched
with excitement. At certain moments in your life, you
just know that everything is about to change. You can
ignore these moments by not acting on the new set
of possibilities they enable, and your life will stay the

same. But if you say yes to their reverberating potential, your life path alters irrevocably. This was one of those unique moments that was about to change everything. I could feel it in my bones.

Everything was coming together in my head. I had to get to my laptop and start typing out my ideas. After the faith forum ended, I rushed back to my place and stayed up all night writing out a lengthy plan for my nonprofit organization. I banged out a list of initiatives I could start with. Hospital feeding initiatives, health related initiatives, potential fundraising ideas, a business card, finding a graphic designer to create a logo, launching a website, ... The ideas kept getting bigger and bigger.

The sun rose, and I hadn't slept at all. Just the mere thought of the speed of ideas that were barraging through my head made me nervous. So I called my mother and spent twenty minutes explaining everything in detail. I respected her opinion more than anyone else's, and I knew she was always looking out for my best interests. Maman would give me brutal honesty. If I could win her over, the idea was a go.

"Oh, this sounds crazy, Trésor, but it isn't the worst idea you've had," she said with a laugh. "I guess it actually makes sense." We spent the next hour pulling my ideas apart. How would I rally funds? Who would join my initial team? The questions went on and on, each one thorough and important. I had a lot on my plate, but the first step was clear. I needed founding capital to get my ideas going.

CHAPTER 11

If it's the Lord's will, it's the Lord's bill

In September 2008, the collapse of Lehman Brothers, a sprawling global bank, brought down the world's financial system. Many still refer to it as the worst economic disaster since the Great Depression of 1929. Times were hard, especially for small less-established ministries such as Mwangaza. Many donors had to choose between donating toward a good cause or putting food on the table. Personally, I was having a difficult time soliciting capital to launch Mwangaza on a wider scale as I had planned.

These times came as I sought to answer crucial questions about my life and the future of Mwangaza. I was coming out of a very difficult season in my life; I needed God to reassure me. Doors I thought were opened were closing one by one, yet I had this dream that God had placed in my heart.

Doors I thought were opened were closing one by one, yet I had this dream that God had placed in my heart.

Meanwhile, back home in Congo, Mwangaza was gaining a reputation. Though the only funding we were receiving was from the money that I made in the part-time jobs I had in America, it sufficed to make a name for ourselves as a microscopic organization that occasionally donated a handful of rice packets to partnering orphanages and hospitals around Kinshasa. We also organized Christmastime celebrations with those who had nothing.

A small leadership team had begun to develop, consisting of those who were acquiring an interest in more than mere participation in our occasional feeding initiatives. Their energy was infectious, their work ethics unmatched, and most importantly, their vision for the organization and its future aligned with mine. We were a ragtag group with one common thread: to build a better Congo than the one we'd inherited. Mwangaza had all the right people in the right positions yet it had not become the story that I wanted to tell just yet. I was still struggling to find capital that could sustain our projects. Creating something new is easy; creating something that lasts, now that's the real challenge.

But through teamwork and dedication, I had a growing faith that our vision could be molded into a reality. I have often heard people say if it is the Lord's will, it's the Lord's bill.

I received a disturbing email from my sister basically stating that if we could not find seven thousand dollars, it would be useless to go forward with any of the initiatives we had planned for the organization. We had been planning to launch an initiative to help rape victims in a small village east of Congo, called Bideka. Because we did not have the money, we were going to have to call off the project.

These were hard times and I knew the only key to getting through this new season was going to be faith.

God was ushering us into a new season where we were required to go beyond what we had been currently doing, yet every time we tried to take a step forward, our efforts were met with obstructions. These were hard times and I knew the only key to getting through this new season was going to be faith. We just had to trust that the Lord would make a way through the surging ocean that threatened to drown us.

Upon receiving the news, I began to search for funds more intensively, yes, desperately, with no response. A friend then suggested I contact the Bible college I attended and ask for a chapel offering. I was reluctant because I was unsure that the offering would be enough to cover the huge need we were facing. Still feeling desperate, I decided to go ahead and ask.

The wait was painful. I painstakingly prepared my

speech to appeal for funds, but two weeks before the chapel service, I received an email announcing a date change. Another fundraiser for an emergency situation in Haiti required an immediate response. I was offered a date that happened on a day when Mark, one of our professors, would be preaching on finances. Initially, I did not hold out much hope for this offering, but once again, the voice in my heart told me to be still, so I kept my spirits up and hoped for the best.

A chapel offering is such an interesting fundraising exercise. The speaker has five minutes to convince college students that the cause he champions is worthy of their giving. I had been writing and rewriting my speech for several days when I received an email from the professor in charge of offerings: the speaker of the day had announced during a faculty meeting that his goal was to raise ten thousand dollars for Mwangaza.

There was at first a flush of excitement reading the email, but then the feeling that it was too good to be true began to overwhelm me. I read the email several times to make sure I was reading it right. Then I called my friend Karl to take a look, in case I had misread. It was true; the goal would be ten thousand dollars. But we had so many questions in our minds. Would the speaker bring people from the outside to come and donate? Perhaps he was going to send out an announcement ahead of time to ask students to bring a specific amount of money for chapel. After all, if you ask 700 students to bring twenty dollars each you would meet the goal. We speculated and wondered, but, again, it was God's plan. In the email, the speaker mentioned that he would need further information about Mwangaza. I swiftly replied to the email and waited for an answer. After two days with no reply, I began to worry. I wondered if the speaker was uninterested in our ministry.

Tuesday came quickly, and it was time for chapel service. I left early that day so that I would be ready in case I needed to make the appeal myself. I walked into chapel and Mark, the speaker of the day, told me to find a place to sit. He assured me that the college family was going to give a nice offering. My friend Karl had joined me that day and we were very curious to see how the service would go.

Soon it was time for the sermon. The sermon was very brief. Mark mentioned an opportunity to give to the women and children in Congo. He said he was not going to pass the offering plate. Karl and I looked at each other, wondering where the ten-thousand-dollar offering would come from. After all, how do you raise funds if the offering plate does not circulate? Mark was on stage holding an offering plate. He reached into his pocket and dropped in two items. He then issued a challenge to the school. Everyone was to return to their dorm rooms. They were to look at their excess and choose something they did not need and bring it back to the chapel. Mark's idea was to have an eBay auction. The whole idea was that if we got rid of some of the things we didn't need we could fund an entire ministry and change lives all the way into the heart of Africa.

Something special was happening on Ozark Christian College's campus that day. It was powerful, and it was about to impact the lives of countless people all the way in Congo.

A heavy silence fell as he began to tell the students about the needs. Then one by one they began to leave. Very soon the chapel was empty. I looked around and Karl and I were among the only people left. Frontline, the college's worship band, was singing praises to the Lord in the empty sanctuary. Something special was happening on Ozark Christian College's campus that day. It was powerful, and it was about to impact the lives of countless people all the way in Congo.

Karl left, and I stayed there by myself, singing with Frontline. I do not remember how long it took, but students began to come through the chapel doors. One by one they came with things that were precious to them. They carried these items like an offering.

Soon a long line had formed leading to the stage. They placed their offering on the stage and returned to their seats.

I was in awe of what God was doing in our midst that day. It was impressive to me that, though they were displaying so much joy, they were giving up things that were valuable to them. Their faces glowed with joy. They smiled as they walked back to their seats. Some seemed so relieved when they were walking back. This was such a powerful example of joyful giving. Once everyone had placed their items in whatever space that was available on stage, they joined in the worship.

Praises rose to our Lord. I had been a student in the school for five years and had just graduated the semester prior. I knew most of the students. I knew they had given up things that were important to them. Yet, arms high and in one accord, they were singing to the Lord. I had heard that chapel singing countless times before but never like they sang that day. There was something special, and all of us could feel it. Mark then came on the microphone and thanked the students on behalf of the women and children of Congo.

The giving did not stop that day. Chapel remained open for off-campus students to bring their offerings. The stage was so full there was nowhere to step. So much "stuff" was given that it took an entire dorm room to store it. The students were wonderful. Some of them gave their time and organized everything needed to make sure it would be listed correctly on eBay. Items sold very quickly, the financial goal was reached.

I was filled with joy and saw God's provision far beyond my expectation. Though I could say that I have seen His provision in many unexpected ways, this was new. Our Lord is the God of surprises. The offering at Ozark Christian College was not just a financial blessing, it was a gate opener.

Our ministry entered a new season. The Lord blessed us with all we needed to build the foundation of Mwangaza as we know it today.

I will always remember the day Mark Moore handed me the check. He said, "This is the Lord's money. Be faithful, brother, and change lives!"

These three truths remained in my heart. It is the Lord's money and He gives us resources for the vision He places in our heart. We are to be faithful with what is entrusted to us whether we are in the days of humble beginnings or in the season when provisions flow. When God gives a vision, He provides everything good to advance His kingdom.

Our ministry entered a new season. The Lord blessed us with all we needed to build the foundation of Mwangaza as we know it today.

CHAPTER 12

The defining moment that led me to my purpose

Long before receiving the chapel offering at Ozark, God painted an extraordinary vision in my heart. In it, I saw flashes of glorious green mountains wreathed in mist. I saw a giant lake on the foot of the hills. Then I saw a group of women—Congolese women clad in traditional flowing cotton dresses. It was just a quick glimpse, but I felt petrified. That discomforting feeling didn't leave, it troubled me for days. I've never underestimated the power of vision for I've always believed that visions are the source of hope: a vision births purpose and can change lives.

Some of the Bible's greatest breakthroughs started with a vision. Noah escaped the great flood because he followed a vision. Moses freed the people of God from slavery in Egypt because of a vision. God's mandate to me was clear; He was calling me to start a ministry—more specifically, a ministry for the women of Eastern Congo. Receiving the chapel offering from Ozark was a reaffirmation that I had to take the next step to the east. There are no coincidences. God always puts people where they need to be.

Traveling to the eastern provinces of Congo would not be easy. The entire region is highly inaccessible. Although there is an international airport located in Bukavu, almost no planes land, due to the persistent volatility of the area. Eastern Congo hosts a medley of Congo's deadliest armed rebels.

In 2002, Joseph Kabila signed a ceasefire agreement to end decades of war. As part of the stipulations, he appointed two rebel group leaders vice presidents of Congo. Other groups, however, remained unconvinced that the agreement would bring results that favored them. They violently resisted integration and camped out in the dense forests and tiny villages in the east, gradually building an army by kidnapping, looting, killing, and raping thousands of innocent civilians.

To make matters worse, many warlords in the region were said to be re-arming. In just a few short weeks, Congo would be making history. After forty-six years of authoritarian rule and protracted violent conflicts, Congo would hold its first multi-party general elections. For the people, the upcoming elections signified the hope for a new and prosperous Congo, free from violence. For the rebels, Congo going to the polls was just another reason for them to spawn violence.

I believed that running toward what scared me the most meant running towards the thing that fueled me most, my destiny.

Before I left Kinshasa, my father warned me that the eastern region was unstable and that potential conflicts could erupt at any given moment. My mother was afraid I would die there. My friends, who had connections in the secret services, also told me not to go. They all told me that my visit to the east was taking place at the worst possible time. Yet I was determined to go no matter what. It did not mean that I was unafraid. I was scared to death at the mere thought of coming face to face with any aggressive militia groups, but I was determined to overcome my fear. I believed that running toward what scared me the most meant running towards the thing that fueled me most, my destiny.

My friend Christian, one of our volunteers, decided to go with me. He braved his fears and stood by me in faith as I carried out my vision to expand to the east. I will forever be grateful that I had Christian by my side during the trip.

There are no accurate words to describe what I

felt when I landed in Kavumu International Airport. It was a mixture of joy, anxiety, and fear. I was back in the city of my birth, back where the first lines of my life were written.

The airport in Bukavu shares nothing in common with modern airports in the west. It has no tower, nor does it have a building to welcome the passengers. Everyone had access to the plane, and there was a crowd outside. My cousin Jean Pierre picked Christian and me up from the airport, along with another companion.

As I was walking out of the airport, I walked past a street boy, lying on the floor with a container of coins in front of him. I felt a powerful nudge in my heart and was reminded why I was there in Bukavu.

The airport is forty-five minutes from the city itself. The military presence was apparent in every corner; soldiers were patrolling with heavy weapons in their hands. Billboards and posters calling to vote for party candidates were plastered far and wide. The upcoming elections were in every mind. We happened to enter Bukavu at the same time as two of the candidates.

Roads were blocked. Traffic was building as crowds gathered along the road. Everyone cheered for Vital Kamerhe, a native of the place who was running for parliament. Shortly thereafter, another group of cars came through; this time the crowds booed and shouted insults. It was Jean Pierre Bamba, running against Joseph Kabila for the presidency. It was obvious that Kabila at this point was still Congo's darling. All of Bukavu was unleashed; people could freely express their support and there was no violence, just high-spirited citizens passionate about what was happening in their city.

As a Congolese I felt lucky to be alive at such a time as this, to witness, for the first time in history, millions of Congolese practice their right to decide their nation's future.

Over the next few days, we travelled from village to village, meeting with churches and community leaders. I wanted to understand what was happening before making a decision. Everywhere I went, people lived in unbearable conditions. The war had taken everything away from them.

The further we drove out of the city, the fewer people we saw on the roads. The looks on their faces, too, drastically changed as we drove further out. They wore a look of fear as they watched our vehicle drive past them. In an instant, you understood that you are now in dangerous territory, where people lived in fear. The Interahamwe, a Rwandese militia reportedly responsible for the genocide, was still actively operating in these areas.

After a long journey through the hills, we reached a quaint village on the top of the hill called Kidodobo. It is a place of amazing beauty. The buildings in the area were built during the Belgian colonial era; some of the buildings still reflected its colonial splendor. The most prominent building is a large white villa that has been turned into a church. There were large windows surrounding the top of the villa and a huge tea plantation surrounding it. The air was fresh, to the point that made us almost forget we were in militia territory.

Their *kikwembe* (Congolese dress) covered their heads and shielded their faces from the light. I recognized their dresses; these were the same dresses that I had seen in my vision.

The pastor met with us and gave us a tour. The building behind the church was a youth center. Missionaries in the past had turned a plot of land that once boasted an Olympic-sized swimming pool into a building for a children's orphanage. The pastor told us that there were no more children in the orphanage; they had to abandon the children's project due to insufficient funds.

On the other side of the church sat a clinic. From the outside, the clinic had clean white walls and maintained its colonial elegance, but inside were people suffering from all sorts of illnesses. Most were sick with malaria. As we were visiting the different rooms, we passed a group of ladies. I initially assumed they were sick, but something about them caught my attention. They sat on a bench, heads bowed. Their *kikwembe* (Congolese dress) covered their heads and shielded their faces from the light. I recognized their dresses; these were the same dresses that I had seen in my vision.

I asked the doctor accompanying me what had happened to them.

"They are VSV," the doctor replied. He explained that "VSV" is an acronym that stands for victims of sexual violence. "Some of these women have been gang raped by fifteen militia men. They have been through the most horrific experience one can imagine."

I recalled a story my father had told me about a girl from the east who was sent to Spain for a medical procedure. She had been so brutally raped that her insides no longer held together.

These women were physically hurting; they were at the clinic to receive treatment for their physical conditions. But what about the hurt we could not see? The pain they would not talk about? I wanted to speak to these women but was not sure how. After a moment of hesitation, courage grew inside of my heart. I asked the doctor if I could speak to them.

"Sure," he replied.

I went up to them, introduced myself, and told them I was visiting the clinic for research. I told them that I wanted to know more about them. They were hesitant at first. They merely lifted their heads and stared at me blankly. There was a long pause. No one said a word.

Then a lady in yellow spoke first. She told me how she was raped in front of her children. Ten militiamen took turns raping her. They used knives and sticks, then inflicted pain that she said was 'indescribable."

As she spoke, the other women mustered their courage and began to share as well. Their lips trembled as they spoke. It was petrifying to hear of such atrocities.

I felt chills all over my body, and the trauma that I thought had been erased from my life came rushing back. I began having flashbacks of men violently beating people; sounds of weapons being fired went off in my head.

Share our story so that people may know what happened here. No woman must live through what we have lived through.

I took a step back and was about to walk out to get some fresh air when the lady in yellow grabbed my arm.

She lifted her eyes to meet mine, and told me in Swahili, "Share our story so that people may know what happened here. No woman must live through what we have lived through."

I left the clinic that day with a heavy heart. The words of the lady in yellow kept pulsating through my mind. Before I left Kidodobo, I stood at the top of the white church's stairs and looked out into the beautiful lush green hills.

The stunning view contrasted with the dark story I just heard. I had gone through such a rapid and profound transformation within that short conversation with those women. Purpose can manifest itself in so many different places, through so many different experiences. That was the defining moment that lead me to my purpose. I knew exactly what I had to do.

After that visit I sent out an email to my team. I told them that I had found a location to plant our first ministry, in Bukavu. We were going to commit to provide rehabilitation and refuge for women who were victims of sexual violence.

CHAPTER 13

Victory
for Congo

I returned to Ozark in 2008 to finish my final semester. With every conversation I was having about Mwangaza, it began to feel more real. I was meeting extraordinary people and having more inspired conversations.

The people around me would be my driving force to help get things started. I had to find a community in Joplin that I could be part of. I had to stay connected and keep networking.

There was a young man in Bible college named Chad. His friendship was and is such a blessing to me. Chad was working on his thesis for his master's degree; the focus of his thesis was John 17. Chad opened my eyes to a deeper meaning of community. He explained to me how, as Christians, we are a united group of people doing life together because we are connected on an individual level with Christ and others. The name of Jesus connects us and makes us family.

My conversation with Chad made me realize that the people around me would be my driving force to help get things started. I had to find a community in Joplin that I could be part of. I had to stay connected and keep networking. That was how I was going to get Mwangaza off the ground in America.

Several families around Joplin had adopted children from Congo, and we connected through social media. They often asked me questions about Congolese food after coming across pictures of the traditional dishes I would cook and share on Facebook. Just like Kathy, they wanted to cook these dishes for their adopted children. I thought I could compile all these recipes by writing a cookbook. It would also be a way for me to preserve and record all Maman's valuable family recipes that I'd grown to love through the years. My friends reminded me that to produce a cookbook meant professional pictures to accompany the recipes, not just those I had been taking with my phone camera. I had recently made friends with a group of wonderful artists in Joplin who were part of the Local Color Art Gallery. I asked them to join my side project. My proposal was simple. I cooked the food, they took the pictures, and together we savored the food.

Thus began a weekly gathering every Monday to enjoy fine Congolese cuisine and share personal stories about what God was doing in each of our lives. We became like family and I began to find comfort in our time together. Eventually, more joined us. But the regulars were Margie, Sue, Jesse, Becky and the talented Priscilla who took some beautiful pictures of the food I would prepare.

In the midst of writing a cookbook and focusing on grad school, an old friend from my time at Ozark Bible College called me one fine evening. Dave, who had become like a brother to me, was aware of my passion to help the people of Congo. He told me that he had a great fundraising idea and suggested that the funds collected through this initiative be directed to aid women in Congo.

Dave was also an established Zumba® instructor and explained to me that a Zumbathon® could be a great fundraising initiative. He explained that a Zumbathon was an event that gathered people for a few hours to dance and simultaneously raise money for a good cause. "People do it all the time in America," he said.

The idea was great, but we needed a suitable venue. Dave suggested that an ideal place would be the Victory Ministry and Sports Complex, but neither of us at that time knew anyone who worked there. So we decided to put the idea on hold while I carried on with my weekly Monday cooking gatherings. One day over lunch, I casually shared about the prospective fundraiser, adding that the Victory Ministry and Sports Complex would be an ideal venue for it.

Becky, a woman who had grown to nurture and care for me like a mother, was a woman with kind eyes, a strong heart, and a laugh that could light up any room. Who knew that she was to be the monumental missing piece that would connect me to the team at Victory? She happened to be friends with the leaders there and gladly shared their contact information with me. Once again, this was no coincidence, but all part of God's providence.

I got in touch with Becky's friend at Victory to set up an appointment and a week later received a call back proposing a date. I was a nervous wreck that next few days. Becky told me, "If you have butterflies in your stomach, be grateful. You are in a wonderful place. If it scares you, just run toward it, because at the other side of your nervousness, there's almost always a God-given opportunity, and this is your chance to seize it."

> If it scares you, just run toward it, because at the other side of your nervousness, there's almost always a God-given opportunity.

I found Becky's friends Jeff and Misty, the leaders of the Victory Center, to be the warmest husband-and-wife duo. The faith and authority they carried when they started to speak instantly impressed me. Both of them listened with great interest as I shared my countless stories and my crazy dreams.

What began as a conversation about how we were going to put together a Zumbathon turned into a twenty-four-hour prayer event for Congo. "Victory for Congo" was born. The idea was to gather the community of Joplin, just before the event, and engage in prayer for Congo. We had no idea how many people would come, but we were going to go forward with promoting it and hope for the best.

As we started planning for Victory for Congo, I stayed up each night cold-emailing everyone in my contacts to promote the event. The response we received was tremendous; many pledged their support to attend the prayer event and the Zumbathon thereafter as well.

It was a moment of unity when worshipers from all

over town came together to worship the Lord and to pray for their brothers and sisters in Congo. I felt so blessed to see so many people who had never been to Congo or even heard of it come together in unity and love to support the event.

It was a sight to behold, one I will never forget, when the worship leader began to pray for Congo and for Mwangaza. He was calling out all these things that held the country in bondage and breaking them in the name of Jesus. All of us began to pray and sing, praising the Lord for the victory in Congo. We praised Him that His name would be proclaimed in that troubled land. I believe that our prayers broke the chains and laid out a foundation for a new season of change in Congo. The prayers proclaimed that day also brought a clearer perspective on the vision I had for Mwangaza.

After the all-night prayers, the Zumbathon happened and funds were raised to build Mwangaza's first-ever Hope Center in Kinshasa. The vision for the center is for it to serve as a hub for all future Mwangaza community development projects. We now had a building of our own. Birthed by the prayers of His faithful children in Joplin and fully dedicated to the Lord, the Hope Center would help propel our ministry into a new season. I saw John 17 happening at Victory for Congo. Unity in love and compassion from brothers and sisters just as Jesus prayed in John 17. It was a true testimony that Jesus is Lord.

As for me, I experienced the promise of Mark 10:29. I gained countless brothers and sisters. I gained mothers and fathers and children. I believe those who came experienced the same thing. Our children and our communities began to pray for the family of believers in Joplin. A divine connection that reminds us that through the blood of Jesus we are one. We belong to each other.

What a picture of heaven as believers come together as one to pray for each other and worship the King. We are each other's reward, and it is a promise for this life. We left everything to follow Him and the gift He has for us is family. May we truly experience this blessing of fellowship with each other and with God so that our joy may be complete.

CHAPTER 14

Bringing Hope to Kinkole

It is often said that for people to understand the magnitude of a need, they need to see statistics, pictures or even videos. These are vital to describe the vast scale of various social crises. Without them, the logisticians trying to deal with the issues will never be able to call the shots. I spent a lot of time thinking about the separation of data, figures and real people.

Often we appeal for donations and funding by listing big numbers and feel as if it will make an impact, but humans can only process data to a certain extent. Only once you get on the ground can you actually start seeing those towering numbers in terms of real people with tragic stories. I have always placed an emphasis on the phrase "seeing is believing." Only when you witness something with your own eyes do you begin to get a sense of the magnitude of a need in raw, human terms.

In 2006, I went back to visit DRC and became acquainted with a ministry in Kinshasa that took care of people living with HIV/AIDS. The ministry took me to a place called Kinkole, a small rural village that is part of Kinshasa district.

Only when you witness something with your own eyes do you begin to get a sense of the magnitude of a need in raw, human terms.

Kinkole is known as Congo's holiday town. On Sundays and holidays, Kinshasa's elite would descend to this little "holiday" town to drink beer, eat the country's best liboke de poisson (fish cooked in banana leaves) and listen to live music. It is a town that relies on urban tourism. Which also means the entertainment action starts around midday, but peaks after dark.

While on vacation, people often take risks they would not usually take at home. They tend to drink more, use drugs more, and generally be more adventurous. These adventures very often also involve taking sexual risks. Due to the extreme poverty, many women and girls in the community succumb to having commercial sex as part of a survival strategy for themselves and their dependents. For this reason HIV/AIDS continues to be a growing epidemic in Kinkole.

During my visit, I came across an entire community of people that were living with HIV/AIDS. It was a shocking experience for me to see how even young children were battling the disease. The visit taught me that the magnitude of the epidemic among babies and children was directly related to the transmission of the infection among adults, particularly women of childbearing age.

One particular girl caught my attention during this visit. She followed us everywhere as we toured the area. Inquiring about her, I learned she was HIV-positive and therefore did not have long to live. At the time of this visit, treatment medicines called ARV were scarce in the area and not readily available for children like her. Unfortunately, she succumbed to the disease and passed away about a year later.

Though I did not have the chance to know this little girl, personally learning about her condition was heartbreaking for me. Something needed to be done to help these children! Food, clothes, sanitation—they lacked the basics. Their eyes were filled with sadness. They were battling excruciating physical, mental and emotional pain that was far too great for their tiny bodies to withstand. The ministry that had been taking care of them through the years struggled to meet their basic needs. Most grants had run out and they were unable to find new partners to cover their expenses. I told the Lord that I wanted to help these children.

The Lord then led me to a small church in Oronogo, Missouri, who decided to partner with Mwangaza to help meet their needs. We started from giving gifts to children that Christmas to regularly providing a meal for them every Thursday—the only meal some of the children were receiving. The First Baptist Church of Oronogo would go on to become a partner that never gave up on the children. Over the years, they continued to love and provide for these children whose faces were filled with hopelessness. Through their continued partnership, each Christmas became a special affair. The despair and sadness the boys and girls had borne for so long turned to smiles and celebrations.

The First Baptist Church of Oronogo would go on to become a partner that never gave up on the children.

After that very first visit to Kinkole, I learned to love these children as I watched them grow. I learned about their lives, their stories, what they liked to eat, their hopes and dreams. I spent countless days and nights brainstorming with my team, trying to think of new ways to make a lasting difference in the lives of these children I had become so fond of. After much deliberation, we decided to plant our second Hope Center in Kinkole.

I signed all the necessary paperwork to officially start construction. Like the Hope Center in Kinshasa, the center in Kinkole will serve as a safe environment for the children to play, learn, and strive to become self-sufficient individuals in the community. It seemed a full proof plan.

What I really desired was to empower these children with monetary opportunities to make a living for themselves.

It took a few months after construction of the Hope Center officially launched till a solid shape took form. Wooden planks were nailed down, future walls had been outlined with strings, and an entire community was preparing for the big moment our Hope Center would be up and running.

Yet I felt as if there was a piece missing. We had no solid program for the children to partake in, once construction was complete. Sure, the children would follow the standardized school syllabus, based on what the Ministry of Education in Congo had implemented, but what I really desired was to empower these children with monetary opportunities to make a living for themselves. An unexpected opening eventually came up around a quaint Mexican meal in the small town of Carthage, Missouri.

I was introduced to Rick and Tammy, a lovely couple, by Misty, a leader at the Victory Ministry & Sports Complex in Joplin, Missouri. Tammy is an artistic person who produces unique art pieces, and I had an idea to collaborate with her to produce pattern templates that the children could use to make handbags. This could create possible job opportunities for these children.

I explained my idea to Tammy over some sumptuous Mexican dishes. "The idea is for the girls to weave your pattern templates into handbags that can be sold to people in America."

Tammy thought it was a great idea and was instantly keen to lend a hand toward making my idea feasible. She agreed that by providing these girls with job opportunities, they would be able to rise above poverty and create lasting, sustainable changes in their lives and for their families as well. As we conversed, I extended an invitation to Rick and Tammy to join me on my next trip back to Congo. Both have a heart for children. They dream of raising a generation of children who will love the Lord.

"Come to Congo and meet these children, and get to know each one of them. Each of them has a unique story to tell. You will grow to love them as much as I do, I'm sure of it. Being immersed in the life of these children will be the best way to see, experience and walk in the shoes of those we are called to serve. It will be a powerful reminder that we are all the children of God."

Both Rick and Tammy agreed. I was excited for the stories the Lord was preparing to write through this trip to Kinkole. It would be special in many ways, but mostly because I was about to embark on a lifelong friendship with Rick and Tammy. God was taking us to a place to change the story. A place where defeat would be turned into victory.

Preparations passed quickly and soon Rick and Tammy were on their way to Kinkole. We began our journey bouncing around dirt paths and visiting communities that had been deeply affected by HIV/AIDS. Poverty was rampant. Families lived in mud huts, some corrugated tin-shacks, a few in basic cement homes. Electricity and running water were luxuries. Children in tattered clothes milled about, eyeing us curiously.

Amid all this, our Hope Center in Kinkole was slowly taking shape. There was a flurry of activity at the center. It had become a place of refuge for the community living around the area. After-school lessons were taught to children with HIV who had been ousted from regular schools. Regular meals were available to kids who usually had not even one meal a day to eat. Then an elderly woman approached me to say how she had been waiting her whole life for a place like this.

I had pictured this day for some time now, but this was a far more powerful feeling than anything I could have anticipated. The center was the dream I had for my people in Congo, and it was happening right in front of me. The feeling of elation was indescribable.

As we spent the day playing games with the children, I announced that Rick and Tammy were our new partners. I told the girls how they would be working on a new project weaving bags using pattern templates that Tammy would design for them. The joy on their faces that day was priceless.

When I first met these children, it was impossible to get them to smile. They lived in constant fear of death. They never dreamed of a future and they had no ambitions. Even those around them reminded them that death was imminent, that their lives were worthless. The news that they would be collaborating with Tammy gave them hope to have ambitions and aspirations to strive to be.

Because they know how it feels to be loved, they can smile. Their songs are now songs of joy and victory.

Today, when asked about their ambitions, the girls would respond that they want to be doctors, bankers, pastors, some even determined enough to envision themselves as the future president of DRC. God has truly taken the children on an amazing journey. Now they know what it feels like to be loved unconditionally. Because they know how it feels to be loved, they can smile. Their songs are now songs of joy and victory.

As we were about to end our visit for the day, I noticed the absence of one of the girls. Upon inquiring about her, I was shocked and saddened to hear that she was pregnant. One of the leaders went on to explain that an older neighbor had raped her. I was devastated.

These children were very much like my own, and to hear that a daughter was raped made me sad and angry at the same time. One of the toughest parts of an open center program is that you do not always know what happens to the children once they return home. The neighbor noticed that she was vulnerable and took advantage of that. Nothing was done for her to receive justice.

After our time of fellowship, our leader suggested that we pay a visit to our little girl. To protect her identity, I will call her Elise.

Her house was a little drive from the center. Kinkole is near the Congo River so most people make a living by fishing in the river. They have no running water, so they go to the river for all their needs. The same water they drink serves as a dish room, laundry room and bathroom.

Due to the contaminated water, waterborne diseases are rampant. As we drove by we could see the face of poverty in the area. We saw people who could barely feed themselves and their children. Most homes do not have fathers because they have gone fishing or they are just not there. Children grow up in an environment where they are vulnerable.

Amid all the social issues you see in Kinkole, children who are victims of AIDS are at the lowest rung of the community. They are outcasts. Everyone runs away from them. When they are rejected by everyone, they have no protector, and they become vulnerable to all sorts of abuse such as what happened to Elise. So many thoughts were running through my head for such a short drive!

> When they are rejected by everyone, they have no protector, and they become vulnerable to all sorts of abuse such as what happened to Elise.

We soon arrived in her neighborhood, where there were several shacks in which families of ten or fifteen lived. We walked through two compounds to arrive at the house. People stared at us, wondering what we were doing there. When we arrived, we found her family except for her father and brother.

Her mother seemed happy and relieved that we came to talk to her; her siblings, too. They were glad that we came to see them and pray for them. We sat and listened to the mother telling us what happened. She told us how abandoned they felt, and how there was no justice for her daughter.

I could not help but be angry that this could happen. It was hard to watch a child I knew since she was little go through what I was hearing. I was so shocked that I forgot to translate for my friends. All my attention was directed toward this baby who was going to be a mother at fourteen.

After listening to the mother, I asked Elise what she wanted to do. "I want to go back to school," she replied with a trembling voice while looking down. She was wearing the same yellow shirt as the last time I saw her. What would her future hold? Her baby's? But there was hope because Christ is greater than any problems we try to solve.

We shared a few words of encouragement with the family. All I could think of at that moment were the promises of the Lord in Isaiah 61 for Elise and her baby: beauty for ashes, freedom for the captive, comfort for those who mourn, a crown of beauty instead of ashes. Before we left, we asked Rick and Tammy to pray for them.

They began to pray a blessing over Elise and her family. I took a couple of steps back while they prayed and observed the prayer circle. Elise's little sister was glowing with joy, and I saw peace come upon Elise. Elise's sister told us at the end that she was happy we came to pray for them. I knew the Holy Spirit was present in that moment and that Jesus' arms were wrapped around this wounded family.

Elise has come a long way since our visit to her home that day. She is back at the Hope Center, catching up on her academic program so she can rejoin a regular school and continue her studies once again.

"Sometimes when I'm alone, I think about the incident, and it's a really painful memory, but I feel so grateful for my child," she says. "I want to be a successful mother for my baby and I know I can do that through Christ who gives me strength."

"I've forgiven him," she says. "For now," she adds.

CHAPTER 15

The hungry
need not wait

A Handful of Rice

There are people in the world so hungry, that God cannot appear to them except in the form of bread.

– Mahatma Ghandi

I have always been fascinated by the story of Jesus feeding the five thousand people that came to hear him speak. How would it have felt to be part of such an event, where so little could be multiplied into so much? I picture the disciples going around with their baskets, wondering if they will have enough, and yet the deeper they went into the crowd, the more they realized that the food was multiplying and that there would be enough. They kept going, probably tired from walking, and not only did they get enough for everyone, but they had plenty left. What a story!

At the end of each year, I look back and am never sure how the kids were fed. The Lord feeds them because they are his own.

It is impossible not to wonder in awe about a man who could instantly multiply a few crumbs into a banquet. For the rest of us, feeding a crowd that large requires strategic planning and a substantial fortune. I often consider feeding the children of the Democratic Republic of the Congo as my personal version of what the disciples experienced. It has always been a walk based on having faith.

On many occasions we simply do not know how we are going to find the resources, yet it is our charge to trust the Lord that he always has more than enough for everyone. At the end of each year, I look back and am never sure how the kids were fed. The Lord feeds them because they are his own.

George Müller is one of my role models in ministry. Müller was an evangelist in Bristol, England. He cared for orphans in his town. It is said that he cared for 10,024 orphans in his lifetime. My favorite story about George Müller is the story of how he fed the orphans by simply having faith.

One morning, all the plates and cups and bowls on the table were empty. There was no food in the larder and no money to buy food. The children were standing, waiting for their morning meal, when Müller said, "Children, you know we must be in time for school." Then lifting up his hands he prayed, "Dear Father, we thank Thee for what Thou art going to give us to eat."

There was a knock at the door. The baker stood there, and said, "Mr. Müller, I couldn't sleep last night. Somehow I felt you didn't have bread for breakfast, and the Lord wanted me to send you some. So I got up at 2 a.m. and baked some fresh bread, and have brought it."

Mr. Müller thanked the baker, and no sooner had he left, when there was a second knock at the door. It was the milkman. He announced that his milk cart had broken down right in front of the orphanage, and he would like to give the children his cans of fresh milk so he could empty his wagon and repair it. George was truly a man of faith. He had no money of his own. God provided for every one of his needs without him having to make appeals or even having to work to find the resources to care for the orphans.

Everywhere I go in Congo, I am asked for help to feed the children. Schools complain that children are unable to pay attention in class because they are underfed. In some villages, I find children too hungry even to move, let alone smile. Their heartbreaking situations often leave me feeling hopeless. It is then that I use what I call the Müller method. I thank the Lord for the food that is not there and believe that all will be fed!

From the very moment God planted a seed in my heart to serve the people of Congo, He has consistently made a way for us to carry all our projects through to completion and, as a result, Mwangaza has been expanding exponentially. In 2015, after much deliberation, the entire team had come to the consensus that we were ready to expand our work to another area of Congo, wherever the needs of the people were greatest. We foresaw that God was about to test our faith through this expansion project.

Looking for potential sites for our next center, we came across the quaint little town of Kisenso, perched on a ridge affording breathtaking panoramic views of Kinshasa City. Many paved roads lead up the hill, where sits the office of the Kisenso commune. (Communes are the equivalent of counties in the USA.) As we drove past this well-painted office, paved roads came to an end and the real face of Kisenso appeared.

Towering mountainsides filled the skylines, but on the ground, little children with tattered clothes carried jerrycans filled with water.

Roads were in terrible condition, filled with trash. The bustling markets swarmed with people walking through the trash to buy what they needed. Malnourished children with swollen bellies emerged from the mud huts and excitedly waved at our passing vehicle. We pulled up on the side of a street to quickly survey the area. As I walked along the street I was captivated to see the extreme poverty juxtaposed with the spellbinding views of Kinshasa from the hills.

Towering mountainsides filled the skylines, but on the ground, little children with tattered clothes carried jerrycans filled with water. Kisenso is a place one would describe as hopeless, a slum with no urban planning.

One million people live in that area without clean water and almost no access to health care. Education is a luxury. Kisenso, according to the Congolese Ministry of Health, is one of the worst places to give birth in Congo. The precarious economic condition of the area, added to a hub for poverty, breeds all sorts of explosive violence. Children are the first victims. They are exposed to all sorts of diseases and violence. They also face hunger every day.

I asked a little boy where he was going. He stopped, gave me a smile, and shyly explained that he was going to get water from a well.

I gave him a large bottle of water that we had in the car but continued to talk with him.

Delighted with the bottle of water, he eagerly introduced himself as Jacques. He explained that during the dry seasons it was hard for him to get to school because he had to wait a long time for his turn to fetch water from a distant well. He could only fill his bucket halfway lest it be too heavy to carry. He makes two trips a day so there's enough water to go around for his whole family.

Jacques also explained how his family had instituted food rationing. "Because there isn't enough food for everyone, we take turns eating," he said. "I eat on even days; my siblings eat on odd days. Today is an even day. So I've just had my meal and now I have to fetch water for my family."

On odd days, he only had water to drink. He often walked around in search of fruits on those days. "If we had water here, we could easily attend school without fail," said the little boy. He thanked me for the bottled water.

As I watched little Jacques heading for the well, jerrycan in tow, I thought about how the lives of the children in Kisenso are consumed with finding water. Because they are deprived of so basic a thing, a commodity many of us take for granted, many women and children are unable to live up to their best potential.

Before we left that day, I decided that I had found the ideal place for our third Hope Center. Back in my room that night I wrote an email to the rest of the Mwangaza team to say that I expected us to expand to Kisenso within the next few months. We would need to raise a lot of money to make it possible, but the first step would be to acknowledge that God would make a way for us.

Meanwhile in Joplin, Missouri, Mwangaza had officially been adopted as official partners of the Victory Ministry Sports & Complex. An online fundraising portal was set up and an overwhelming amount of pledges and donations were pouring in from all over the world through this platform.

It felt so surreal to watch Mwangaza grow from just being a vision that I had to help the children of Congo to now having a top-notch digital fundraising platform putting its full weight behind our expansion to Kisenso at no cost to us.

The entire team celebrated when we received the news that funds had come in to make our plan a reality. It was the culmination of everything we had been through as an organization.

Each of us on the team knew at this moment that we were participating in something bigger than anything we had done so far.

The validation we had worked toward had finally come about. All the late nights and meetings, the tiny wins, and many obstacles had made this sweet moment a perfect celebration. Each of us on the team knew at this moment that we were participating in something bigger than anything we had done so far. We had been blessed with a unique opportunity to create remarkable change in our community, and we were on our way. The groundwork had been laid out; now it was up to us to follow through.

In just a few months, the Hope Center in Kisenso was on the verge of completion, and I went back to Kisenso with Rick and Tammy specifically for the Tuesday community meeting. These weekly meetings convey a wealth of information and amazing opportunities for ministry. As we gathered at the nearly complete Hope Center in our Victory Room—aptly named after the Victory Ministry &

Sports Complex in Joplin—I felt a sense of gratification and reflection swell up inside.

Every person at Mwangaza had felt tremendous pride in the scope of our impact over the past few years. We had exceeded every single expectation others put before us—and outshot our own ambitions as well. But if reaching peak performance is difficult, maintaining it is nearly impossible. We knew we needed help in our next phase, so we called in the community to tell us what they needed. Based on that, we would make our next set of plans.

The community explained to us that because of the lack of opportunity they did not always have the means to feed their children. They did not want a handout or anything of the sort. They wanted work so that they would be able to feed their children. The people believed in the work we did, and they wanted to support it by learning skills. Keeping this in mind, we decided to put together a kids camp.

This would be our version of the ministry I had seen done in Arlington, Texas. I was so impressed by the community outreach in Arlington that I had long wanted to adapt the concept to the realities of the Democratic Republic of the Congo in general and Kisenso in particular. Teams would go out to neighborhoods in the slums and reach out to children through games and sports. The Hope Center would serve as a base for this children's camp.

We decided that the objective of the camp, in addition to a program carried out for the children, would be an avenue for us to provide the community with hands-on involvement in the work that we do. The camp would help them learn practical skills that would generate sustainable livelihoods for themselves and their families. This would benefit the entire community around the Hope Center in Kisenso.

After countless nights and days intricately planning the events of the camp, the day finally arrived. Children gathered at the Hope Center ready for the day's events. They had their beautiful camp shirts and looked nice in their outfits. My mother got up at four o'clock in the morning to cook enough food for one hundred people. Chez, our ground staff, helped her cook. They made delicious chicken, beans, and rice. For the majority of the children, this would be the best meal they would have in a while. When the time came, we carried the food to Kisenso and joined the party.

The road to the Hope Center is in such bad condition that it does not allow access to our gate. Nor did we have the right kind of vehicle to drive through the rough terrain in front of our property. We had to park one street back and carry the food along the narrow pathway. Once we started unloading, the smell alerted the children in the area. It was only a matter of time before a huge crowd of kids was following us. They were hungry and wanted food, but the food we had was for the hungry kids inside the gate. This was one of the hardest walks to take. It felt as if the short walk to the Hope Center was suddenly miles long.

They walk by you, they hold your hand and try to flatter you, just so they can get some of the food to fill their starving bellies.

One by one the little ones climbed the wall. They stared at those inside eating and begged for even a little bite of chicken. It was hard to fully enjoy the time with our campers because my thoughts were fixated on those begging for food. The joy of the children inside was mingled with the heartbreaking cries of those at the gate.

We collected the leftovers hoping to feed a few at the gate. Obviously, not much was left because the children inside were also hungry. They barely left any food. It was hard to have enough for even ten children after the campers were done.

After thinking of ways to feed them, it was time to leave, to walk through the crowd with empty pots.

The crowd of little adorable children begging for a bite was hard to face. They look at you as if you had forgotten them. They walk by you, they hold your hand and try to flatter you, just so they can get some of the food to fill their starving bellies. The reality was that we were carrying empty pots and that there was not even a handful of rice left.

The real danger of ministry in the Democratic Republic of the Congo is the feeling of being hopeless and helpless in the face of certain situations.

That evening, my friends Rick and Tammy asked me why we left so fast. They thought perhaps I had sensed danger and that was why I rushed everyone out of the area. I felt helpless in the face of the need. This is probably what the disciples felt when they came to Jesus to find a solution for those who were hungry. I identified with them in my walk to Jesus with my empty pots.

People often ask me if Congo is dangerous. Yes, it is dangerous. The real danger of ministry in the Democratic Republic of the Congo is the feeling of being hopeless and helpless in the face of certain situations. The overwhelming needs of the people, the meager resources on hand remind us of the disciples' plea to Jesus, "Lord, increase our faith!"

A man in Missouri once showed me the statistics of orphaned children in Kinshasa. I was presenting at his church and praising God that we were feeding one hundred children. The man approached me at the end of the service with a smile on his face. I was expecting to hear something encouraging from him but when he began to speak, his words were tainted by discouragement. He said, "There are thousands of children living in the streets in Kinshasa. Do you feel like you are making a difference by only feeding a hundred?" He went on to add, "Don't you feel like this is a failure?" These words have come to haunt me several times in my work.

These are painful moments in ministry when the words of one man cause me to question all the work we do. I think about this almost daily in my current position at Mwangaza. But it is important for me occasionally to take a step back and reflect upon all the victory that Jesus has given us. I look back see how the Lord has miraculously turned a handful of rice into the three-and-a-half tons of food we regularly distribute today. That in itself has been quite a triumph in our mission to eradicate hunger in Congo.

Thanks to the collective efforts of various humanitarian aids and responses, tens of millions of people in Congo have been able to rebuild their lives after the war. While the headlines can sometimes be disheartening, as a person who follows global hunger trends for a living, I can tell you this with absolute certainty: *We are winning the long game in the fight to end hunger.*

CHAPTER 16

Grace abounds in the deepest waters

Each person comes into your life for a purpose. Everyone you meet will have something valuable to teach you. Some will leave an indelible mark in your life, some will bring out the best in you.

The year 2007 was a year when I was plagued with despair and a life-limiting condition. It was during this time that I met Dr. Paula. She saved my life with her unsurpassed skills as a doctor. We often talked about her visiting Congo.

Some of my fondest memories in life involve sitting on the shores of Lake Kivu with my siblings, throwing small stones into the clear, aquamarine water and watching the sun light up the ripples we made.

Eight years later, what was just small talk became a reality. Doctor Paula and her husband Floyd finally decided to pay me a visit in my home country. Our initial plan was to go to the Équateur province in northern Congo. Dr. Paula was interested in the Pygmies. After much consideration, we decided to collaborate and launch a project that would benefit the Pygmy people. Équateur is home to the Pygmies and to Congo's lush and sprawling rainforest, the second largest in the world.

However, getting there got a little more complicated than expected. As we were working out the logistics for the trip, we learned that transportation and road conditions made it impossible to make it to Équateur. Given this roadblock in our plans, I offered to take Dr. Paula and her husband to the East instead; the Kivu region, to be more precise.

The beautiful eastern provinces of Congo are home to an incomparable wealth of biodiversity: rare trees, tropical birds, and some of the last gorillas on the planet. I had not visited in many years and was looking forward to rekindling memories with people who mean so much to me.

Some of my fondest memories in life involve sitting

on the shores of Lake Kivu with my siblings, throwing small stones into the clear, aquamarine water and watching the sun light up the ripples we made. I remember being struck by the smells of the morning mist surrounding the stunning mountains. There is nothing quite as fresh as that.

So much anticipation and preparation led up to this trip, even the slightest hitch in our plans would have been a major letdown in retrospect. Our little hitch began when we received word that Dr. Paula and Floyd's flight was canceled, causing a ripple effect on our overall schedule for the trip. To make matters worse, the Belgian airline that was supposed to transport us to our destination was severely delayed.

I stood in the arrival hall, staring at the screen as several flights kept getting delayed. Then it dawned upon me that we were going to end up staying the night at the airport. Anyone that has been to the N'Djili Airport in Kinshasa would know that there are no hotels around the airport.

I sought places for us to stay the night, but the only place that was offered to us was in one of the business lounges.

When Dr. Paula and Lloyd's flight arrived in Kinshasa, I had to be the bearer of bad news. "Our connecting flights are all delayed. Looks like we'll be using the couches at the business lounge as our makeshift beds for tonight," I told them, hoping they would take it all in stride.

True enough, both Dr. Paula and Lloyd, no matter how tired, told me that they were all in for an adventure and were more than willing to rough it for a night. They were such troopers.

Each of us found a comfortable spot to sleep for the night in the business lounge. Just as we were all bundled up and slumped out on different couches, I tried to make a joke out of the situation. In a deep, commentary-like voice I announced, "Ladies and gentlemen, we are about to embark on a Lord-of-the-Rings-like adventure. We are to form our fellowship at the N'Djili Airport, Kinshasa. Instead of destroying an evil ring, our mission, should you choose to accept it, will be to spread love in the eastern province of Congo."

Thankfully Dr. Paula was the first to raise her hand and gleefully declared, "I accept!" Everyone burst into fits of laughter before finally closing their eyes and turning in for a brief nap. Our night was short: check-in was 5:00 am.

Approaching our gate, several large floor-to-ceiling windows overlooked the wide-open space surrounding the airport. I saw the sky breaking and the sun slowly making its way through the dark clouds. I thanked the Lord for a new day and for all the new opportunities coming our way.

We made it to the plane, all five of us. My sister Rose, Joelle, Dr. Paula, Floyd and I were all cozy and belted in our seats when the pilot announced that we were waiting for hot water to be delivered to our plane. We were stuck in the plane for another hour before we could finally take off. Once we did, Joelle cried out, "Finally!" and the rest of us had a good laugh, considering the back-to-back delay we had been facing.

Our route was Kinshasa to Goma, via Kisangani. Once in Goma, we were to take a boat on Lake Kivu to Bukavu, where we were to make our way to all our ministry sites. It did not matter how we did it, all that mattered was we did it. After all, when deciding to set out on a journey, it is not necessary to know how you will arrive at the destination, just that you will.

Flying into Kisangani is always special. The Swahili and Lingala language regions meet there where the Congo River merges into the rainforest. The view from the plane gives a wonderful glimpse of this miracle of nature. As we flew over the airport, I couldn't help but think how significant this place was to me. My life is bound to the city where my mother was born, my parents met, and my grandparents are buried. I have prayed over the land many times.

Once known as the martyr city, Kisangani now calls itself the city of hope. There are deep wounds in the hearts of the people. I prayed as we flew over the city that God would heal the open wounds still destroying lives in that eastern part of the Democratic Republic of the Congo.

After a short layover in Kisangani, we took off for Goma. Due to our delayed departure, we landed an hour late and we—and several others on the flight—would have to rush not to miss our boat ride. A church leader assured me on the phone that he had spoken to the people at the port: the boat would not leave without us. We gathered our luggage and ran through the arrival hall to get to our waiting vehicle. We knew we had to beat the crowd. With the number of people at the airport, I was taking no chances. Unfortunately, when we arrived, our boat was gone! After all that mad rush, we still missed the ride.

Our only two options were to spend the night in Goma and try again the next day or to board a "night boat" and arrive in Bukavu that evening.

The prospect of taking the night boat frightened me. The night boats in Congo were notorious for making headlines: "The motorized boat was traveling at night without lights, hit a rock, and capsized." Just the thought of it brought shivers to my bones. But it was crucial for us to get to Bukavu as soon as possible. We were already behind on our schedule; any further delays might mean aborting the entire mission trip. We had no choice but the night boat.

We headed to the Port of Goma. My first impression was that it looked like a cemetery for old boats. Very large crowds of people were milling everywhere. Young men walked back and forth, offering to carry our luggage. Once they learned we were thinking about the night boat, everyone wanted to help. Two boats were leaving that night. The first boat looked as if it might just sink upon launch, the second little better.

"What do you think?" I asked Floyd.

"This one seems better," he replied, pointing at the second boat.

We asked if we could take a short tour of both boats so we could decide. The second boat had an option where we could have a room all to ourselves. For an extra fee, we could get a cabin with four life vests. In fact, the sole life vests on the boat were available only for passengers in the rooms. Business class, on the other hand, also looked relatively nice, with a flat-screen TV and comfortable furniture for about thirty guests. We decided to go with that boat.

The closer to departure, the more people came to first class. By the time the boat sailed, there were probably ninety people altogether in business class. There was no room to walk and to stand up meant to lose your seat. I took it upon myself to protect everyone, so I stayed put throughout the voyage in the crowded room and watched over the cabin door.

In the business lounge people talked about music, alcohol, politics, and everything they could think of, until they were too tired to talk. The room quieted as they fell asleep on each other's shoulders.

That night, I made a new friend, a veterinarian at Kahuzi Biega National Park. We spoke a lot but mainly focused on the severely endangered species of silverback gorillas in Congo. We also briefly talked about cultivating apple products. Then, around 1:00 am, he told me something that set off my anxiety.

The port in Bukavu does not open until 7:00 am so we were most likely going to float on Lake Kivu for about thirty minutes. For a man who does not know how to swim, the thought of an overcrowded boat floating in the middle of a large lake was just plain scary. Nor did it help that I had watched the TV show Lost before I left America. My mind was filled with all sorts of scenarios that could go wrong.

I decided not to let fear overcome me on such a special journey. I embraced the truth that God is in control. He reminded me of His presence in the beauty of the lake and His protection when I saw the strength of the mountains. He reminded me that He takes care of every living thing. I opened my Bible and read a passage from Psalm 107:

"Others went to sea in ships, conducting trade on the vast waters. They saw the Lord's works, His wonderful works in the deep. He spoke and raised a tempest that stirred up the waves of the sea. Rising up to the sky, sinking down to the depths, their courage melting away in anguish, they reeled and staggered like drunken men, and all their skill was useless. Then they cried out to the Lord in their trouble, and He brought them out of their distress. He stilled the storm to a murmur, and the waves of the sea were hushed. They rejoiced when the waves grew quiet. Then He guided them to the harbor they longed for."

In all my moments of fear, I have learned to cry out to the Lord and leave it to him.

– Psalms 107:23-30

In all my moments of fear, I have learned to cry out to the Lord and leave it to Him. He brought me peace as I observed around 5:30 in the morning that the dark skies were giving way to the first rays of daylight. The sun was rising. I saw the light pierce through the darkness. God reminded me of the meaning of the word "Mwangaza": a light that breaks through darkness. I knew it was a sign and a message that hope is rising in the east. God protected us and led us to the harbor we longed for that night. At 8:00 am we finally made it to Bukavu. We were tired but thankful to the Lord that we made it.

CHAPTER 17

Finish what you start

Our Mwangaza leaders were waiting to welcome us on our arrival in Bukavu. We only had enough spare time to drop our luggage by the hotel before leaving again.

Our first destination, Bideka, is a special place for me. Eight years before, I had a life-changing experience at a small hilltop village called Kidodobo after meeting a group of women that had been brutally raped by members of the militia. It was after that visit that I plunged into a partnership with a clinic to help women who were victims of sexual abuse. That partnership officially commenced Mwangaza's first ministry in eastern Congo and that has since expanded to a nearby village next to Kidodobo called Bideka.

Now here I was, eight years later, bouncing up and down the familiar dirt roads, valleys and hills. Through the years, I traveled these paths numerous times, gradually watching the young girls that first joined our programs as victims grow into independent, strong women of faith. They have come a long way and the mere thought of how God had healed them from within brought a smile to my face. These roads brought back so many bittersweet memories from my past adventures.

I never saw the lady in yellow from the clinic in Kidodobo again. I have searched for her many times and asked around but to no avail. I think of her every time I return to Bukavu; her story left a lasting impression on my life and changed me forever. Wherever she is, I wish her peace in her soul.

When I first started the initiative with the clinic, our goal was clear. We were going to work toward helping victims of sexual abuse rebuild their lives, their bodies, and their future. Through the years the team did their part and provided constructive support toward those in need. Today these girls are no longer girls, they are grown women.

They prayed for husbands and God gave them husbands. They prayed for homes and now have built their own homes. Sure, their homes are not big or beautiful, and they still must survive on an income of less than a dollar a day, but the crucial point is that they are no longer victims. They are survivors.

Very often when running a humanitarian aid project, a leader may feel compelled to cling to an idea that we initiated. The decision to move on can be difficult even in the best of times. But when the work is done, the best thing to do is to simply close the loop. And that was precisely what I was planning to do on this trip to Bideka.

At the clinic, the doctors and nurses came out to greet us. The clinic is the only place of hope in the area. People walk miles to receive help there. I stepped out of the vehicle and took a deep breath. A pleasant scent wafted from the nearby tea plantation. Women worked in the distant fields. They were only tiny figures at a distance but seeing them was a testimony that the land that once witnessed human brutality was alive again. God's healing hand was at work there.

We were ushered into the clinic's meeting room. The girls I had been looking forward to seeing were waiting for us. I introduced Dr. Paula and Floyd. They were delighted to see us, but I think I was even more delighted to see that these girls were now women. They had their children with them.

"Here are your grandchildren," they told me. I was taken aback to be referred to as a grandfather. Not in a million years would the thought of being a grandfather have crossed my mind. But these girls looked up to me as their father figure, and I had watched them grow from strength to strength as if they were my own daughters. In that moment, I embraced the thought of being a grandfather. It was truly an honor to be a grandfather to these little ones, and I was swelling with pride.

I announced that my partnership with the clinic had

come to an end, and that we would be moving forward to help other girls in their same plight but in a different location.

The girls were thrilled. They shared how the program had empowered them with life skills they would use to pursue business opportunities in their town. After a few songs and gift presentation from our donors to the kids, we left Bideka to return to Bukavu.

All I could think of was to praise my God. My King in His infinite love gave me an opportunity to see the fruit of faith. Two generations are growing to know Him in Bideka. His name is lifted high.

"Your kingdom is an everlasting kingdom; Your rule is for all generations. The Lord is faithful in all His words and gracious in all His actions."

– **Psalms 145:13**

CHAPTER 18

These are the dreams of our children

Bukavu is an interesting place. The name Bukavu means "the place of few people." It has grown exponentially and is now the largest city of the east. Nestled along the gorgeously contorted shoreline at the southern tip of Lake Kivu, Bukavu is truly a sight to behold.

As we drove through the mountains, our view was filled with lush green hills overlooking the lake. The bright sun reflected off the still waters of Lake Kivu as we reached the township that perches on the steep hills. Dr. Paula at one point insisted she saw a hippo mother standing in the water, nuzzling her child. It was breathtakingly beautiful. Young children walking down the streets waved at us as we drove past. Time seemed to stop altogether at such sights.

Whether at the greatest level of affluence or the deepest level of poverty, parents always desire for their children to have a better future than theirs.

In all my years on the road, I've never encountered a region combining such an intense blend of beauty, potential, and energy with misery, horror, and cunning. Bukavu is undeniably a rebel-held town, surrounded by jungles that are besieged by militia groups. As a result, huge numbers of rape cases are reported—women and young girls are increasingly preyed on by local soldiers and other militia group members. Despite the heartbreaking realities, there is hope where there is a willing heart, and there were many willing hearts in the community.

In my travels, in countless conversations with parents while their little children played around us, I always asked, "What would you like most in this world, if you could choose anything?" expecting to hear "a less corrupt government," "new roads," "a better job," or "peace," but always getting the same response: *an education for my child.*

No matter their situation, whether at the greatest level of affluence or the deepest level of poverty, parents always desire for their children to have a better future than theirs. I truly believe that nothing can more profoundly unlock a person's ability to change his or her place in life than a quality education. Recognizing this, we decided to concentrate on getting the seven million absentee primary school children in Congo back to school. It was a big, audacious goal for us as an organization, but each of us could comprehend the magnitude of impact this could be for the people of Congo.

This trip to Bukavu was primarily to visit different schools in the east to get a better idea how to kick start our mission plans. Rainy weather had made our journey unpleasant, dirt roads had turned into mud, and our van could go no further. Here we met a representative from a mission organization in Bukavu who would lead us to visit a school located in the slums. We had to walk the rest of the way. We passed by cardboard houses, some made with only a few pieces of wood as a foundation. These homes housed ten or more people.

Groups of children began to follow and to greet us, calling out that "bzungus"—Swahili for white people—were visiting. They were fascinated that Floyd and Dr. Paula were walking on the same road with them. Each of the children smiled and enthusiastically welcomed us to their humble neighborhood.

Atop the hill was the school. The director greeted us very graciously and kindly. As she led us on a tour, she explained the basics: how many classrooms they had, which ages the school served, and how far it was from town. I saw that the classrooms were built of wood so flimsy and old it could fall apart at any moment.

An average of sixty-five students shared a little classroom. The director explained that the jug by each student backpack was to spray the ground so that dust did not interfere with their learning. It made sense, then, why respiratory diseases kill so many children in the area. Toilets were a luxury at the school.

Three hundred kids had to share two toilets.

As we made the rounds, I heard giggling coming from one of the classrooms and peeked in. Unsupervised, three little girls were practicing their letters at a chalkboard. Unaware of me, the oldest whispered each letter as she watched the other diligently write it on the board. They then took turns to write and practice their alphabet. As I approached to join them at the chalkboard, they huddled together in embarrassment, covering their mouths to hide their laughter.

I picked up a piece of chalk and gently wrote my name, Trésor, on the chalkboard. I then pointed to my chest and said in Swahili, *"Jina Langu Ni Trésor."* I handed the chalk to one of the three girls and said, "Now you," and nodded toward the chalkboard. By now, a small crowd of kids had gathered. After much prodding, the girls slowly wrote some letters on the board and gave me back the chalk.

"Denise," she said, and the kids exploded with laughter.

After her, a different child wrote her name, then another, and then another. These children, all by themselves on a hot afternoon, just above the river where their mothers were washing clothes and their fathers were fishing, gathered in this wooden classroom seeking education. All they needed was a safe place, and this school provided that space for them.

Though they were so excited by the sight of our team, especially the strange-looking Dr. Paula and Floyd, in their village, I think I was even more thrilled by the sight of them. Seeing these kids make the most out of the little that they had to learn the alphabet and educate themselves, was a profound inspiration to me. As I stood there in that wooden classroom surrounded by these zesty children, I realized that I had found the first school to plant our next project, right there in Bukavu.

CHAPTER 19

The Forest People

Before the Belgians came to Congo in search of timber, rubber, and metal, eastern Congo was blanketed with woods, and the people who lived there were the forest people: the Pygmies. For thousands of years, Pygmies have lived in harmony with equatorial Africa's magnificent jungles. With only about 250,000 of them remaining, Pygmies are the largest group of hunter-gatherers left on earth. However, today they are under serious threat.

I first heard about Pygmies in history class as a child. My teacher explained that the earliest known reference to a Pygmy—a "dancing dwarf of the god from the land of spirits"—was first found in a letter written around 2276 B.C. by Pharaoh Pepi II to the leader of an Egyptian trade expedition up the Nile. Another reference can be found in the *Iliad*, where Homer invoked a mythical warfare between Pygmies and a flock of cranes to describe the intensity of a charge by the Trojan army. In the fifth century B.C., the Greek historian Herodotus wrote of a Persian explorer who saw "dwarfish people, who used clothing made from the palm tree" at a spot along the West African coast.

For centuries the world has categorized this unique tribe of people as "the others.

More than two millennia passed before the French-American explorer Paul du Chaillu published the first modern account of Pygmies. "Their eyes had an untamable wildness about them that struck me as very remarkable," he wrote in 1867. In *In Darkest Africa*, published in 1890, the explorer Henry Stanley wrote of meeting a Pygmy couple: "In him was a mimicked dignity, as of Adam; in her, the womanliness of a miniature Eve."

Pygmies are notable for—and named after—their short stature. The word "pygmy" derives from the Greek word for "dwarfish." There appears to be a fascination with people whose physical appearance seems bizarre to us, and due to their unconventional physical appearance, for centuries the world has categorized this unique tribe of people as "the others."

Growing up, I was admittedly ignorant about the Pygmies and their culture. On more than one occasion I made inappropriate Pygmy references. My friends and I nicknamed anyone short a "pygmy."

The pygmies have been neglected and oppressed— often even treated as subhuman—in Congo.

If I, from Congo, could be so ignorant toward my fellow countrymen, imagine what the rest of the world thought. In 1906, a Congolese Pygmy named Ota Benga was temporarily housed at the American Museum of Natural History in New York City—and then exhibited, briefly and controversially, at the Bronx Zoo. He was paraded at the zoo, like some kind of animal. Unsurprisingly, Ota fell into a depression and, a few years later, committed suicide at the zoo.

The pygmies have been neglected and oppressed— often even treated as subhuman—in Congo. Dr. Paula had been studying the Pygmies for some time. The main purpose of her trip to Congo was to further study the plight of the Pygmies in order to improve their lives.

To help facilitate Dr. Paula's study, I arranged for us to join an initiative to revive the Kahuzi-Biega National Park, a protected area near the city of Bukavu, named after the two dormant volcanoes within its limits. In 1980, Kahuzi-Biega National Park was officially designated a UNESCO World Heritage site for its biodiversity of rainforest habitat and its eastern lowland gorillas.

Over the past decade, Pygmies have been forced out of their homes in the wild jungles due to the abuse they have suffered from the rebel groups hiding there. The war had been especially brutal for the Pygmies, having endured killings and rape, but even more shocking is that they have also allegedly been the victims of cannibalism by the heavily armed fighters.

As a Congolese myself and a war victim, I have seen and heard of cruelty, massacres and genocides on a shocking scale, but to think of human beings hunted and eaten as though they are game animals, in their own home ground, is in itself is a mind-blowing catastrophe. In times like this, I wonder how we can have fallen so far as God's divine creations.

Pygmies feel they have lost their dignity as human beings and have to rely on other tribes for their daily needs.

This dire situation has left the Pygmies with nowhere to go, and so they have found refuge in the preserved areas such as Kahuzi-Biega. Ironically, their presence in the park has proven detrimental to the environment. The Pygmies, due to their way of life, have a legitimate need for wood and for food, so they have cut a significant portion of the forest that had been preserved.

For generations the lives of the Pygmy have been closely linked to the forests that they consider their paradise. After all, the forest provides them everything they need for life—food, shelter, medicines, and so on. Now being forbidden to live in the reserved parks that take up huge swaths of Congo's forests, the Pygmies feel they have lost their dignity as human beings and have to rely on other tribes for their daily needs.

In many cases, they have been exploited by these tribes, who consider them low-class humans fit only for degrading and worthless work. The key issue here is that these Pygmies have no alternative.

They keep going back to the one place they can trust, doing what they know best. They secretly enter the forests to hunt, to collect medicinal plants, wild honey, mushrooms, firewood, etc., because they desperately need to feed their families. Entering the park is treacherous, because if captured by park rangers, Pygmies are considered poachers and are severely punished for doing the only thing they excel at—hunting.

The initiative that Dr. Paula and I were invited to be part of would provide the Pygmy community incentive to settle outside the park and render the park's forest less attractive. Some of the proposals included providing a steady supply of wood and opportunities for food. But the main objective was targeted at the children. The general hope was that the project would empower the children's role in the larger community so that in the future the Pygmies would not need help to survive but would possess adequate life skills to live a quality life. This is where Dr. Paula and I came in. Our role was to build bridges with local and international schools to sponsor and enroll the Pygmy children so that they could learn to read, write, and ultimately get an education. The opportunity to forge a partnership with the national park could not have come at a better time. Education had now become our primary focus at Mwangaza. Providing every child in Congo an opportunity to obtain quality education will be the strongest foundation for the people to improve the quality of their lives.

So in the months leading up to our visit to Kahuzi-Biega, Dr. Paula, I, and the rest of the Mwangaza team spent days and nights soliciting sponsors who would provide funds to send these Pygmy children to school.

Our efforts were successful; we found adequate funding. We had good news for the Pygmy people and could not wait to share it with them.

Our trip to Kahugi-Bieza National Park began by road, eighty kilometers from Bukavu to Tshibati. We were warned that during the rainy season the road turns to mud. The first fifty kilometers were on nice paved roads, but our last stretch was indeed bumpy and muddy. The roads in South Kivu are always beautiful with trees and green hills. It was hard to believe that these same places were the sites of massacres ten years earlier. The region in the vicinity of Kahuzi-Biega National Park and the national animal research center was once a jewel for research and a tourist attraction. It is now struggling to stay alive.

We finally arrived at Lwiro station, actually a research center under renovation and restructuring after years of damage due to war and looting. Our driver explained that the station was divided into two main sections. To our left was the conservatory area that served as a habitat to snakes and to our right was the home of the glorious silverback gorilla, the most endangered species of gorilla. In awe, we heard these majestic, powerful yet sensitive creatures roam wildly and freely in the protected territories. The park is one out of the handful of places left on earth where scientists and tourists can safely see a mountain gorilla in the wild.

Between Rwanda and Congo, over the past fourteen years, hundreds of gorillas have been killed, possibly due to them stepping on landmines or getting caught in crossfires between heavily armed rebel groups and military forces.

Our driver kept us entertained with a story about a huge snake that lives in the research center. "Five hundred meters long!" he exclaimed with wide eyes. I certainly felt as if I was on a Jurassic Park tour with all the wildlife encounters we were having.

After we finished touring the research center, we arrived at the camp. This is where the researchers and other workers live with their families. It was beautiful in the hills. We came across impressive colonial homes that looked as if they were dissolving into the hills just like a beautiful painting. We could only imagine how beautiful the place would have been before the war, before the conflict, in all its glorious splendor.

Once we passed the camp, the driver announced that we still had a seven-kilometer drive up the mountains before we arrived in

Tshibati. He said this is supposed to be the toughest segment of the trip. The rain did not help either; there was mud in several spots. Four kilometers into the ascent, our vehicle got stuck in the mud.

Luckily our partners in the car in front of us made some space for our group to get into their vehicle. The trip was a lot easier in their vehicle. We quickly reached the top of the hill. The view was splendid, with beautiful waterfalls free-falling from the heart of the forest abyss far below. What majestic beauty in the middle of the forest!

They felt connected and bonded with their sponsors who encouraged them to study hard and reach for the sky.

We saw an abandoned mansion far off in the distance. It would be hard to miss: such a huge mansion, literally falling apart. Our driver told us that it was once the property of the king of Belgium. Long ago, before the wars, when the Belgians ruled Congo, the king used to come out into the mountains for vacations. Despite its shabby exterior, the mansion intrigued us: it held a fragment of Congo's past.

We finally arrived at the project headquarters, situated at the peak of the mountain. Our sponsored Pygmy kids were waiting to meet us there, as invited. Each of them had received personalized back-to-school gift packages from their sponsors in Joplin before we arrived. The packages contained brand-new school uniforms, backpacks stuffed with stationery and an encouraging letter that each sponsor personally wrote for the children. The children welcomed us with bright faces and side smiles. Their gifts had given them the confidence that they belonged in society. Their curious parents, teachers, and others from the pygmy community were waiting for us as well. The place was packed.

One mother told us that she "cried and cried" when

she saw the gift that was sent for her son. After introducing themselves, the children read us the letters they received in French. They shared how they felt connected and bonded with their sponsors who encouraged them to study hard and reach for the sky.

After hearing from the children, our hosts gave us a tour of the new sector where Pygmy families are to set up their homes, and we heard their hopes and dreams for the place—so much to do and so much to pray about. As we left, they had a special request. The local women, Pygmies and Bantu, asked if Paula could take a picture with them. These women do not like having their picture taken, which made this request very special. I am convinced that the women saw something in Paula. Somehow, they read her heart and knew that her genuineness was a message. It was Christ's love letter to them.

"The Spirit of the Lord God is on Me, because the Lord has anointed Me to bring good news to the poor. He has sent Me to heal the brokenhearted, to proclaim liberty to the captive and freedom to the prisoners...."

– Isaiah 61:1

CHAPTER 20
Brenda's Victory

"Isn't the fast I choose: To break the chains of wickedness, to untie the ropes of the yoke, to set the oppressed free, and to tear off every yoke?"

– Isaiah 58:6

Very early on in the ministry, I encountered the ugly face of human trafficking at a place called Paka Djuma. You can call it the red light district of Kinshasa—though there are no lights there, just trash. It is a slum where trafficked girls end up in Kinshasa.

I had become friends with Helene, the director of a ministry called BOMO that ministered to these women. As the years passed, I realized the ages of the girls rescued by BOMO were dropping dramatically, down to girls as young as ten years old. The BOMO home gave them a chance to know the Lord and learn a life skill that they could use in the outside world.

In 2007, I met a young lady there. To protect her identity, I will call her Brenda. She was a teenage mother living at BOMO. Meeting her opened my eyes to the horrors of human trafficking.

Brenda was from the southern province of Katanga, two hours flight from home. This was all she knew, because she had been stolen from her family by a child trafficker when she was only seven years old. She told me her story while sitting on the floor. Her eyes seemed lifeless and midway she would get lost in her thoughts. Only by God's grace was she able to recollect whatever fragments remained of her memory to tell her story.

□ □ □

Before her life was interrupted and shattered by her kidnapper, Brenda was a normal seven-year-old. Her father was in the military and her mother sold goods at the market. Since the army did not pay him enough, her father sold wood at the market to make money. Her parents were not married, which made her social standing in the community awkward. She often stayed at her grandparents, who lived in town and worked at a local mining company. Brenda helped sell wood as best she could. She never went to school, because there was no money to.

One day her mother sent her to buy cornmeal and bread. When she arrived at the little store, the men sent her to the store across the street. After crossing the road, a lady approached her to ask where she was going. She remembered the lady telling her that the cornmeal in that area was bad and that her mother would be unhappy. She offered to help her find a better quality of cornmeal. Brenda thought it was a good idea and followed her. Little did she know that it is meetings like this that can change a child's life for the worse.

They walked all day that day. Five other girls were picked up throughout the day from different locations. When night came, the lady brought them to the city hall. Homeless people often slept there. She told the children that they would return home by plane the next day.

In the middle of the night, Brenda was awakened by the other children. They were trying to escape while the lady was gone somewhere. Brenda had often dreamed of flying in an airplane; she was so close to her dream and didn't want to miss that, so she told the other girls that she would stay. Another girl was so sick that she could not go anywhere, so she stayed as well.

Only when they landed did Brenda understand what was happening to her. It became obvious that she would not be going home.

The next day they moved to a home next to the airport where they spent another night. On the third day, the lady took them to the airport. They boarded a military plane as members of the woman's family. Only when they landed did Brenda understand what was happening to her. It became obvious that she would not be going home. They were picked up by someone else, another member of the military, who kept them until the lady arrived. From that point on they were being prepared to be sold as sex slaves.

At first, they were used as beggars. Every evening there was a set amount of money they had to bring back. If the money was not there, they were beaten. Physical and sexual abuse is common in the life of a street child in Kinshasa. When the time arrived for them to be sold, a family member recognized her and set her free.

She was taken to a charity that was to find her family and reunite them. She was blessed to be placed in a foster family. The mother at the house truly loved her and even wanted to adopt her. She felt loved and thought that everything would be all right, but the heart of men is corrupt.

The foster father raped her multiple times. As a result, Brenda became pregnant. She was only thirteen when she learned about her pregnancy. The pregnancy caused strife in the family, so they decided to abandon her. She stayed on the street for a while before a guard at BOMO noticed her.

At the retreat, Brenda wrote on her notepad that her prayer request was to be able to return to her hometown and hopefully find her family.

An arrangement was made so she could come live there temporarily. She had a baby boy, but BOMO was not the place to raise a child. She could only be there for a year. She eventually found a good orphanage that could accommodate her and her boy where she now lives and raises him. She is going to school and helps to take care of the younger kids at the orphanage.

Though she has found a home and is doing a great job at raising her child, overcoming the past has been a trial for Brenda. For a long time, she had a hard time loving her child. The circumstances made it difficult for her to accept him. She lived in anger, frustration and the thought that God did not love her. In 2013, she went to a retreat called "The Heart of the Father." There she understood the heart of God and His unfailing love for her. She decided to forgive those who had wronged her.

She decided that she would be a better mother for her child. At the retreat, Brenda wrote on her notepad that her prayer request was to be able to return to her hometown and hopefully find her family, so she could have closure and really move forward to the next phase in her life.

❑   ❑   ❑

Brenda's story of transformation resonated with me deeply. When you live in a war-torn country like Congo, you grow up with an understanding that conflicts and instability can destroy anything and everything at any time. Families, childhoods, lives– all these suddenly feel temporary, liable to be taken away at any time.

Just when you start thinking that it is useless to have hope in the midst of such experiences, you meet the survivors that come out on the other side, very much scarred but stronger than ever. You learn that the only thing that enabled people like Brenda to survive and then radically change their lot in life were through the strength of their willpower and with the help of others.

Having that smallest, slightest, window of opportunity that can change the course of someone's life forever.

Yes. They all need help to get through life's obstacles, just like I sought for and got help that eventually changed the course of my life. The more I learned about the challenges each one of these survivors had to endure, the more I grasped the importance of having that smallest, slightest, window of opportunity that can change the course of someone's life forever. When one is given an opportunity, staggering personal transformation is possible.

Recognizing this was my inspiration to work toward creating opportunities for victims of human trafficking. I knew I had what it took to empower girls like Brenda to rebuild their lives and to move past their battered old scars, so I decided to organize a conference with the objective of creating a network of people working toward eliminating human trafficking in Congo.

Organizing a conference requires a tremendous amount of forethought and execution, but I had a good support team; we soon worked out our list of invites and selected our panel of speakers. All were individuals representing organizations that were actively advocating to end human trafficking around the world. There was one particular couple, Tom and Tonya Overton, whose careers I had been following for some time now.

They are the directors of Hope 61, an organization that trains and equips churches worldwide to understand the issue of human trafficking, to identify what causes people to be vulnerable to it, and to discover the gifts, talents, abilities, and resources that God has given each church to lessen the vulnerability of those in their communities. I was eager to bring the Overton's training program to Lubumbashi where we had decided to hold the conference.

Lubumbashi we thought would be a perfect venue; after all, it was situated at trafficking ground zero. It was a perfect treat for us when the Overtons agreed to participate as our key speakers. We went ahead executing our plans one by one to ensure all aspects of the conference would go smoothly. I sent my sister Joelle to Lubumbashi where she met Pastor Mwembo, who became our key contact on the field.

He helped spread the word among church and community leaders. Everything was ready. We were well ahead of our deadlines, and everything seemed to be going just according to plan. I could not help but feel a huge sense of pride for the team and their efficiency.

As much as I had held the original vision of Mwangaza, it was my team's support that gave it its legs. Each of them had poured their heart into each of our projects. Regardless of how big or small it was going to be, they just believed it was going to make an impact. It is this belief that has enabled the organization to move forward despite all the obstacles we have encountered. Very often in the world today, we glorify founders and visionaries, when in fact the early adopters and the support system, the team behind the scenes, are actually the ones that make an organization's success possible.

Just when I was feeling most confident, I hit a roadblock. I had failed to prepare for any unforeseen circumstances. I had no plan B in case everything we'd worked so hard to create went awry. At the final hour, the Overtons, our main speakers for the conference, ran into a complication and informed me that they would be unable to attend. We had not booked any other speakers and were at a loss as to how we were going to carry on with the conference. The next best option was to have me speak, but I did not have much experience in the field of human trafficking. This was, after all, a new venture for us.

Human trafficking was a new field for me, but I had met many victims, and each had a powerful story to tell. I decided to share their stories, especially Brenda's transformative tale. It was the first day of the conference, and I thought Brenda's story would serve as an ideal illustration of the evils behind human trafficking.

As much as I had held the original vision of Mwangaza, it was my team's support that gave it its legs.

While telling the story, I noticed that the listeners were staring at me as if they were being emotionally torn apart. They told me afterward that human trafficking was like a plague in their towns. They told of children they knew who had been kidnapped. Hopeless parents organize a funeral after two weeks and consider the child dead. I began to wonder if

153

that is what had happened with Brenda's parents. Perhaps they believed that their little girl was dead.

When the session ended, a participant came to me and said, "We should bring Brenda here. If she comes, she will most likely be able to remember where she came from, and God will allow us to find her parents." This participant's suggestion lingered around in my mind for about two months. Finally, at Christmas, I approached our partners in BOMO and asked to send Brenda a special Christmas gift. We would fly her back to Lubumbashi to help her recollect her memories, find her family, and gain closure. Even if we had to make a series of trips back and forth from Kinshasa – Lubumbashi – Kinshasa, we would look until we gave her the closure she sought. This was our commitment to Brenda.

I would stare at the map, intensely focus on the area within the red circle, lost in my thoughts that somewhere in that vicinity was the place I had come from."

Brenda was thrilled to receive her Christmastime miracle. She told us how, when she lived at BOMO, she had a map of Congo on her wall, and circled the area around Lubumbashi with a red marker. "I would stare at the map, intensely focus on the area within the red circle, lost in my thoughts that somewhere in that vicinity was the place I had come from."

Even though Brenda had now settled in a comfortable home, a home that held greater opportunity to pursue an education and provided a safe space for her to raise her baby, she was still constantly haunted by the memories of the life and family she had lost.

I had promised Brenda that we would help her find her family, but looking back I have to admit that we had little hope of success. We were unsure where to look, or even exactly what to look for. On the flight from Kinshasa to Lubumbashi I asked Brenda why she desired to find her family. How would finding her family bring her closure?

Her eyes took on a faraway gaze as she considered this. "It would have been different if I knew my family did not really love me, and they had possibly arranged to sell me off to the lady. Perhaps because my family did not have enough money to feed all my siblings, and one had to go, and somehow, I drew the short straw. But it was not like that. I never felt that, though the thought crossed my mind many times. But I don't think that. I really strongly feel in my heart that it was just an unfortunate event. I was kidnapped, and my family I feel have been searching for me, all these years."

We had to try. Perhaps, somewhere in Congo's second largest city, among the busy roads and bustling life, was a secret we could unlock.

Brenda's coming to Lubumbashi was an event. Everyone who had attended the seminar wanted to meet her. From the moment we touched down at Lubumbashi, the signs were clear, this was no ordinary undertaking. Despite the non-stop heavy rain, the muddy roads and the road closures, people in Lubumbashi were still persistent about meeting Brenda and reuniting her with her family.

> I was kidnapped, and my family I feel have been searching for me, all these years."

The meeting was held at the United Methodist Church, a place that has witnessed history for 104 years. The old edifice stands tall and elegant as if watching over the city. It is surrounded by schools and other ministries of the church. People are walking by all the time. It is a busy place. We did not know where to go. We roamed around, looking at the different ministries until we received a phone call from our contact, one of our mostly volunteer investigators.

As we drove, rain poured from a darkened sky. The driver told us stories about the city, while I looked around anxiously, wondering how the day would end. I did not want to see Brenda disappointed. We certainly did not come all the way for such an outcome. We prayed in the car and committed Brenda's heart to the Lord. Her hopes were high, and nobody wanted to disappoint her.

When we arrived at the small chapel I was amazed by the place; I wondered how many services it had witnessed and how many prayers had been sent up from those old pews. These questions brought me back to the reality of that day. We were there to see Brenda's prayer answered.

Just about an hour later, Brenda was sharing her story in the chapel. It was her time to make history in that place. I had never seen her so passionate. I had heard her story countless times before, but there was something special about this time. Brenda had hope. She had hope because she saw these people listening to her, knowing they were willing to help. As she spoke, I could see the hope in her eyes and hear the confidence in her voice. She concluded by saying, "Now I am ready to find my family and tell them that Jesus helped me survive."

A deep hush fell on the room when she finished. Some were in tears, others were shocked. A respected church leader promised that the group would find her parents. Her story gave them a ray of hope that some of the children who had disappeared from their city were alive and even trying to find their way home. The group decided to send out more people to different places she remembered, hoping that we would have more clues about where to start our search. So they went, and we stayed at the chapel, waiting for news.

For two hours, we waited, while I anxiously prayed for the Lord to send us an answer. The rain began to lighten up, and the dark clouds gave way to a beautiful sunshine.

Our investigators come through the gate but had little to say. The city had changed. Brenda mainly remembered the market near her house—the market where she got lost. There were gaps in her description of places she remembered here and there; after all, her information was fourteen years old. But Brenda was confident that fragments of her childhood remained vivid in her memory.

"Just take me there, and I'll show you the way to my house," she kept repeating.

She gave us three familiar landmarks. "There is a bridge, a bus stop, and the house on the other side of the street." These are extremely general landmarks, but our search team wanted no stone left unturned. We took her to every possible bridge in town, but her memories still remained hazy. Every step we took felt as if on overlapping film. One film was Brenda's wispy memories, the other the vital reality of Lubumbashi now.

We were looking at each other, wondering which one of us was going to have to tell Brenda that it was time for us to give up the search.

The town had changed so much, and we were seriously beginning to doubt our search efforts. It was getting late in the afternoon. We were looking at each other, wondering which one of us was going to have to tell Brenda that it was time for us to give up the search. I was getting restless and decided that I had to be the bearer of bad news and tell Brenda when I heard her shout from the back of the vehicle, "It's here! It's here!" I looked toward the direction that she was pointing. She was pointing at a dirt road near the railroad.

Brenda wore a stoic expression on her face that reflected the dozens of memories swiftly flickering in her mind like holograms. She insisted we leave the paved road and continue on the dirt road. The dirt road had turned muddy because of the heavy rain that morning. It led us to an abandoned little market. The driver told us that he was aware that there used to be a wood market there. He said that we could be on the right track but didn't remember a bridge on that road. Brenda was still guiding us along muddy roads; we were entering the poorer parts of Lubumbashi.

This place had nothing in common with what you see when you first land in Lubumbashi. Malnourished children with inflated bellies walked barefoot in the mud. This scene was in stark contrast to the beautiful shops and luxury cars we saw in the area around the airport. Poverty was real here. It was in this vulnerable community that Brenda was stolen from her family.

We sloshed through mud, the driver skillfully ensuring we stayed on the little road. "Stop!" Brenda screamed again. "It is that way!" she said, pointing at a little tunnel. It was a small tunnel filled with mud, and we couldn't see the other side from where we were. She was convinced that this is where she was supposed to go.

We stopped and decided to split into two groups, one to stay in the car and another to make their way on foot with Brenda. Helene and I stayed back to protect the car, while our companions went with Brenda through the tunnel. We watched them struggle through the mud until we couldn't see them anymore. Then, all was silent. We were waiting to hear from them, both of us anxiously checking our phones to make sure that we did not miss the call.

I stood outside the car watching little children play. I was sure they had not had a proper meal all day. I thought: *What a perfect spot for traffickers.* Parents were not around, nor did it seem as if anyone was watching over these kids. Just the thought of how sophisticated the trafficking syndicate was in our country made me nervous. I paced back and forth to the entrance of the tunnel to see if I would see their faces. They had been gone for forty-five minutes now and still no news.

In my restlessness, I went back to the car to tell Helene I was going to go through the tunnel and find the others. Just as I did, I spied one of our search volunteers walking through the tunnel. It took him about ten minutes to get through the mud. He bore good news and asked me to follow him to meet Brenda's grandmother.

On the other side of the tunnel was a little bamboo bridge next to a roundabout with a bus stop. A wooden house stood across the bamboo bridge. That's when it hit me that while we had been looking for a modern bridge all around Lubumbashi, the bamboo bridge would have been the only one she knew in town. For a seven-year-old, the bamboo bridge must have seemed rather large.

The volunteer explained, as we walked, how they had asked the other tenants living in the wooden house if they knew a family that had lost their little girl fourteen years ago. Everyone told about an old lady still living there that talked about her missing granddaughter very often. But they were unsure if they wanted to involve the grandmother, lest her hopes be crushed if it turned out that Brenda was not her granddaughter. "She's already been through so much," they told us.

We quickly made it to the house, and I saw Brenda, lost in thought, waiting outside. It had to be quite a moment for her. She had come so far, reached the home that was permanently etched in her memories, yet no one could quite recognize her.

Everyone stayed outside, while Helene and I went in to tell Brenda's grandmother that her long-lost granddaughter had returned and was outside waiting to meet her.

She was very skeptical. Brenda's mother had died of grief, she said, and now her husband (Brenda's grandfather) was very sick, and she was the one caring for him. She didn't want to get her hopes high; she'd been through so much pain and disappointment. It would be best, she thought, if she waited for her son-in-law to come home from work.

We offered her money to buy airtime to call her son-in-law so he could handle things. I was reaching in my pocket to give her the money when one of the neighbors walked in without closing the gate. From where we stood, we could see Brenda leaning against a car. I found the money and was ready to hand it to her, but she walked right past me.

Something had caught her attention, and she had ignored everything around her. She walked toward the gate, and we followed her.

As we drew closer what we saw was beautiful. Brenda and her grandmother were locked in an embrace, with tears running down their faces. The grandmother turned to us and said, "This is our blood"—her way of saying that she belonged in the family.

"Our Brenda is back," she said. "The gods have finally answered our prayers. They have brought joy back. They have brought our Brenda back."

Brenda just stood there overwhelmed, tears sliding down her face. She wanted to know if her family looked for her after she was stolen.

Her grandmother told her how her mother had searched for her and eventually died of a broken heart. After Brenda went missing, their family was torn apart with despair.

Brenda walked back into her family house hand in hand with her grandmother to meet the rest of her family. Meanwhile, the rest of us stood outside overwhelmed by this reunification. We were so glad that Brenda finally got to have the closure that she so deserved.

Our time in Lubumbashi was short. The next day, we had to return to Kinshasa, having given Brenda the best Christmas gift we could ever offer. There were a lot of smiles and silence on our flight back to Kinshasa. Everyone was processing the crazy day we had had, and how God had done the unexpected.

When we landed in Kinshasa, I told Brenda to thank the Lord for the experience: now she knew where she came from. She saw the condition in which her family lived. No one in her family had studied beyond primary school and here she was pursuing a college education. Most of them have no relationship with Christ, but Brenda found Christ who has been her strength in the midst of darkness.

Brenda has had a hard life, but God has given her a family of believers from all around the world who love her. She still has a lot to overcome, but she is no longer a victim, she is an overcomer. I don't know where her story will end, but I know that it will be for the glory of God!

CHAPTER 21

No greater privilege than raising the next generation

People often ask me what it was like to grow up in Congo. I always tell them what my grandmother once told me, "To grow up as a child in Congo, according to God's will, is to grow up in paradise. It is because of the will of man, growing up in Congo today means growing up in misery."

For two decades, Congo was an example of what a world without Jesus looks like. After some of the deadliest conflicts in modern history, the country is trying to find peace again. But some places in Congo needed more healing than the rest mainly because they suffered more atrocities than the rest. Goma is one such place. I knew I had a role to play in bringing healing to this land, but I was even more convinced after the Lord used a young man called Yves to interrupt my routine and tell me about his hometown.

> To grow up as a child in Congo, according to God's will, is to grow up in paradise. It is because of the will of man, growing up in Congo today means growing up in misery."

I was in Goma for a vacation some time ago and met Yves, who was actively involved in various education initiatives in Goma. It happened to be Yves's birthday, and so we went to a place known for its wonderful food. "Chez Magalie" is home to wonderful Congolese cuisine. We were enjoying the meal and celebrating his birthday when I asked him, "Where are the vulnerable communities in this town?"

"You only see the nice part of town when you come here," he said. He told me about the different issues facing the people of Goma in the aftermath of decades of war, violence and instability. That was when the Lord started impressing on my heart that a new page in my life in the ministry of Mwangaza needed to be written in Goma.

Yves had mentioned a community in the city, known

for their strength and ability to take care of themselves. He said they had built a school, known as The Itala School, but most children were unable to pay the small fees. After that chat with Yves, I decided to return to Goma and get more involved with the development of the school.

Goma is like a casket made of gold—beautiful on the outside—but it holds a corpse, stinking and rotten.

The school is located in the outskirts of Goma. Just twelve miles to the north is Mount Nyiragongo, the volcano that erupted in 2002, destroying roads and large sections of the city. As we were driving to the school, I was in awe. The sights were magnificent. The lake, the volcano in the background, and the green hills make it an ideal place to take a postcard picture. A huge road goes around the lake. I was captivated by the beauty of what I was seeing.

Yves, who was accompanying me, in his soft calm voice remarked that Goma is like a casket made of gold—beautiful on the outside—but it holds a corpse, stinking and rotten. Yves was right; there has been little peace in Goma. Frequent attacks by rebel groups have made Goma a difficult place to grow up. But at school, the kids feel protected.

Just as we reached the school, our surroundings changed drastically. Everything in that area was covered by solidified lava. The government had developed the nicer, tourist part of town and got rid of all traces of the volcanic eruption, but, thirteen years later, the poor still deal with it. No longer were we in the nice developed area of Goma with its pleasant villas and expensive hotels. We had entered the derelict quarter, where the forgotten live amid everything that reminds them that time in their world stands still and does not advance for them. We were literally driving through a desert covered in rock instead of sand.

Unlike my view from the plane, here there is no greenery. Nothing grows where the abandoned live. There is no color. Everything is gray like the rocks and so was the atmosphere as we drove through. People looked sad. Life seemed to move in slow motion, with no sand or grass for children to play.

We came across the wreck of a plane. Due to inadequate maintenance, airplane crashes are common in Goma. We saw children playing pilot in the wreckage. Our driver explained how that particular crash killed 89 people. Some of the locals refer to airplanes flying over Goma as flying coffins.

The fifteen minutes from the city to the outskirts felt like an hour to me. There was so much to process. What irony that a land so beautiful and so rich would have suffered so much death and destruction.

A few moments later, we pulled up at The Itala School of Goma and saw the smiling faces of our kids waiting for us. Their parents smiled as well. Here was a moment of exuberant life in the midst of the forgotten land. This was why we came. There is always hope.

We walked to the first classroom. The kids were all excited and stood up and screamed, "Good morning, Mr. Visitor!" Their classrooms reminded me of the ones I had when I was their age in Kindu. There weren't enough desks, so one desk had to be shared with as many children as possible. The rest had to make do with benches, which looked as if they would collapse at any moment. The pathways and floors were uneven and rocky. There was no actual ground to walk on.

The children had no choice but to get used to walking on the sharp rocky ground completely barefoot, as most of them had no shoes. In each classroom we visited, we saw the same layout, but the beautiful smiles of the children showed their contentment. "You are bringing us hope," the director said as we walked back to his office. The truth, however, was that they were filling me with joy and hope.

Ten of the five hundred children attending the school were selected to receive sponsorships through our ministry. I felt rather cynical when asking for a list of the most vulnerable children in a school where every child is vulnerable. But we had to start somewhere. These children were asked to stay after school so that we could meet them and present their scholarships in an official ceremony.

Chairs and a small tent protected the attendees from the blistering heat. Some village representatives were also invited to attend. The ceremony kicked off with students marching into the square, singing traditional songs and swaying to the beat of traditional drums. When the music ended, the village deputy announced each of the distinguished guests and spoke of his own journey, emphasizing the importance of his studies. He concluded with one of my favorite quotes: "Education and hard work is the only ticket out of poverty."

After his speech, the sponsored children received backpacks and t-shirts from us and a promise that we would not give up on them. A special bond was forged between these children and those across the ocean who had given them the opportunity to go to school.

> Education and hard work is the only ticket out of poverty.

After the ceremony, I sat down with the village leaders for a delicious Congolese meal of bean stew and fried plantain. Just then, the loud sound of drum beats rang out in the distance. I couldn't see where it came from, but it sounded as if it was emanating from the opposite side of the school.

The village representatives and school staff sat around a large wooden table sharing jokes while sipping on bottled Coca Cola and Fanta, but as much as I tried to focus on the conversation, my mind kept drifting toward the blasting drum beats from the schoolyard.

"I'll be right back," I told Yves, who was sitting right next to me, and slipped away from the table.

I rounded the corner and could hardly believe my eyes. More than fifty kids, ages around five to fifteen, were furiously dancing in the schoolyard, kicking dust into the air, sweat soaking through their uniforms. They were celebrating the ten kids who had been granted Mwangaza scholarships. All ten of the kids were standing in the middle, surrounded by the rest of the group.

They saw me and grabbed my hands, pulling me to the middle of the circle, cheering with delight. No adults were in sight, and without the glaring eyes of judgment around us, for the next twenty minutes I danced harder than I ever had in my life. The noon heat beat down on us, sweating profusely and laughing uncontrollably. As the dust filled the air around us, we celebrated opportunities and hope.

> When you find your God-given purpose in this world, there is a primal energy that will spur you to move, to shake, and to transform.

Dancing with these kids, I looked around and attested that when you find your God-given purpose in this world, there is a primal energy that will spur you to move, to shake, and to transform. I remembered how special the opening of our very first Hope Center was to me, and I realized that it felt as special to our donors who bought the cement, the traumatized mother and hardworking father who laid the first bricks, and to the child who would now learn to read and write from their first book.

We had truly reached a goal that once upon a time seemed unattainable. Even if it was on a small scale, we could see the fruits of our labor and the impact that we had created. Now it was time to stretch our work further. We couldn't just stop now that we had reached our goal; instead, our goal should motivate us to confidently and audaciously move the finish line far off into the distance once again. It's in the space between the known and the unknown where you can craft a vision for the future and then chase it with relentless fervor.

Though I did not exactly know how I was going to navigate the rest of my journey, I already knew that by giving people of all ages and backgrounds an organization through which they could rebuild their stories in return, I was building my story as well. Mwangaza was simply a way to get the ball rolling toward achieving greater transformation in Congo.

The Itala School is a perfect example of what the right opportunities and empowerment can do to a community. The community was so destitute that they had no money to send their children to school. The cheapest school in the city was too expensive for them. They met and discussed what to do, so that their children would not be left out of the educational system. They built the school and found qualified teachers. The children at the school spoke better French than some who went to private school. When we came in, we started a sponsorship program that endowed the school with an income from the school fees we were paying. We helped them add classrooms. But the community remained in charge of the building and maintenance and it was theirs.

Even though other neighborhoods called their school "the vulnerable school" because everyone was vulnerable there, they were proud to have solved a real problem and responded to the need. They were the experts. We came and empowered them to continue this life as a community. Their sole purpose in this project was that their children would have a better chance at life than they did. Their community looks a lot like the community in the book of Acts, a community that does life together. Women in the community were doing business together and empowering each other. They created their little saving groups to help with some basic needs of their community.

I had discovered a community of courageous men and women who wanted to make a difference but just needed a little help to change their world. Today, The Itala School has over five hundred students. For the most part, they are malnourished and without access to health care, but the students have a hunger to learn and want to change their community. We do all we can to help them make their dreams come true. It is their unshakable faith in the Lord that truly makes that community special.

That faith and the prayers of many is what I believe has kept the city alive. Despite all kinds of horrors, smiles shine bright in Goma. By all human standards, Goma should be a town that lives in desperation. Because of men and women like those of Itala, Goma is a city of hope!

□ □ □

The next day we woke early to prepare for our next adventure even though we only had one item on the agenda for that day. Our goal was to visit the ten sponsored children in their homes. We started our visit in a stone desert, at a small shack where a grandmother was raising her granddaughter. Most people don't take the time to visit people in that area. As we drove through the rocks, peoples' faces and their eyes seemed to wonder what we were doing there. They sometimes hesitantly waved at us or said hi to us.

It was a little home made only of a tarp—that was all they had. Rita and her grandmother lived in that place. Our hosts welcomed us to their little living room. They had two old chairs. There was no floor and all I could see was that they cleared some of the rocks, but it was all dust. They were very nice to us though they had nothing to offer. I asked the grandmother about the rest of the family. I was curious to know what had happened to them. Why wasn't there someone else to help raise Rita?

Her grandmother told me how their family went from being a wealthy family back in Rwanda to where they are now. She is Congolese, and her late husband was from Rwanda. They had crossed the border fleeing from the violence. They ended up in a refugee camp where she lived until war broke in the Democratic Republic of the Congo as well. They were displaced once more. Her children were with her most of the time, but the constant need to flee and the lack of food forced them to go north—to hunt rats in the fields for food.

Rita's father left first, then her mother. They abandoned their daughter. It had been five years since she had news of them. A few rebellions had come and gone in that time. The grandmother looked worried telling us about this. She didn't know if they went missing or died.

One thing was certain. Rita's grandmother loved her and wanted the best for her granddaughter. I could see how she tenderly held her granddaughter as she told us about the little girls' parents. They didn't have gifts for us or something to offer to drink, but what they shared with us was a gift of great value. Their love for Jesus was the best gift for us. After we were done with the story about what happened to the little girl's family, she began to share her faith with us.

The reason I am always tired is because I devote the strength I have left to making sure that my granddaughter can go to school,

She is a strong Christian and a prayer warrior. She stood and pointed at a Jesus poster hanging on the tarp that served as a wall. "Know this man?" she asked us. "He is all I have in this world." I saw her eyes watering as if she was moved by some powerful emotions. She told me that she prayed for me during the night. "I told Jesus to bless you and give you a long life." There is so much faith in that woman. She had no earthly possessions, but she had a testimony. She had a story that by God's grace intersected with ours.

The grandmother told us how God answered her prayer for her granddaughter. "The reason I am always tired is because I devote the strength I have left to making sure that my granddaughter can go to school," she said. She told about her little business. She had a small table in front of her house with one stick of sugar cane. That was all she had for survival. On a good day, she made three hundred and fifty Congolese francs, the equivalent of thirty-five cents in the United States. That gives her enough money to buy a little bit of flour and sardines for both her granddaughter and herself.

Feeding her granddaughter was one of her battles. Equally important was her battle for the little girl's education. It was a dream of hers that Rita would be able to go to school in the best condition possible. She always felt as if she had never accomplished that. She told us with tears in her eyes how she would sit at her table waiting for someone to buy sugar cane. She would see school kids come along with their uniforms and backpacks. She would give them some of her sugar cane for free and she would pray that her granddaughter would have the same opportunity.

She prayed each day for a backpack and shoes for Rita. And God had answered her prayers. I was so touched by what she was telling me. I told the grandmother about my friend Shannon back in Joplin, and how she worked so hard to collect these backpacks for these children. There was one particular blue backpack that was destined to go to Rita. Two weeks later she received her shoes. "This is why I stayed up and prayed for you because God answered my prayer for my granddaughter through you."

I came out of that place encouraged by the unwavering faith of that woman. God is good indeed! As we stood up to leave, Rita thanked me and said, "Thank you for coming, God bless you."

We walked back to the car that day with hearts filled with joy but carrying the pain of seeing that the kids were living in such conditions. We visited ten homes that day. Each home had a story, but, overall, the greatest hope was the knowledge that Jesus' story was intersecting these lives and growing in the hearts of these little children. I had no doubt that we were raising the generation that will bring change to Congo.

Epilogue

When I look back on the time all this first began, one thing was incredibly clear from the get-go. I was hopeful and idealistic from the start. I never thought, I hope this works out. I simply knew it would. That's because it went beyond passion and felt more like a purpose. I felt I had been called to serve my fellow brothers and sisters in Congo and that had become my purpose. Purpose is found when you stop thinking about how you exist in the world and start figuring out why you are put on earth, or what you should do during your time here on earth.

From the very moment that first bolt of electric energy hit me during one class in Bible college, I never once questioned whether the organization I would create would make an impact or not. I just knew I had an obligation, after my heart had been healed, to help others find their healing too. After God showed me grace and gave me hope, it was now up to me to find victory among my people. God always has a reason for all things we go through. We are taught the pain of loss, because if we never know it, we have no compassion for others. The terrible pain of loss also teaches us humility that softens even the hardest of hearts, to make a better person of a good one.

Nelson Mandela, who is today known as the son of Africa, was once quoted saying, "Deep down in every human being there is mercy and generosity. No one is born hating another person because of the color of his skin, or the features on his face, or his religion. People must learn to hate, and if they can learn to hate, they can be taught to love, for love comes more naturally to the human heart than its opposite."

The years of war that Congo faced created a deep and lasting wound in my country and my people. All of us will spend many years, if not generations, recovering from that profound hurt. But the decades of oppression and brutality had another unintended effect: it produced strong characters like Brenda, Elise and Rita's grandmother, women and girls with unwavering faith that show extraordinary courage, strength, and resilience that defies the imagination. It took such depth of oppression to create such heights of character.

It is in meeting these characters that I learned the meaning of courage, that courage was not the absence of fear but rather the triumph over it. From the very beginning, I was hopelessly idealistic that transformation would occur. My country is rich in the minerals and gems that lie beneath its soil, but I have always known that its greatest wealth is in its people, finer and truer than the purest diamonds.

As of the date of the paperback publication of this book, Mwangaza International has broken ground in eight locations around Congo. Our Project Hope, known as "Project Espoir" in French, provides a hub for development and human trafficking prevention. Some of our other projects include economic empowerment, medical care, orphan care, and "water is life." All these projects aim to take care of the physical, emotional, and, most importantly, spiritual needs of those who are lost and broken.

Mwangaza International currently employs staff members in each of our locations across Congo.

Our on- and off-site staff work hard to keep the opportunity alive for the old and young of Congo to rebuild their lives in the face of poverty and despair. It is an exhilarating feeling to think about how a commitment that began with feeding a handful of rice packets to hungry children has now expanded into an organization that provides refuge, opportunities and education to children all around Congo. This is no longer just my story, it has become their story too.

Please consider supporting our work by sponsoring a child, or by getting involved in any of our projects at www.mwangazaint. org. Our work has impacted thousands of Congolese and supported hundreds of families. We are filled with hope that with your support we can strive to continuously empower every child with the message that their dreams are never impossible, no matter how difficult their circumstances; after all, there is always a ray of light that shines in the midst of darkness. As long as somewhere in the world, a child still stands with an outstretched hand asking for nothing more than a handful of rice, our mission will continue to shine through to them.

Photos

All we had was a handful of rice, then the miracles began.
We now distribute up to three tons of rice to those
in need around Congo.

*Mwangaza's first ever Hope Center stands strong
today in Kinshasa.*

Dedicating a well at Life Hope School, Kiswishi.

*Christmas time celebrations with the children is now an
annual Mwangaza event in all the regions we serve.*

Among the different facilities available at our Hope Center in Kisenso is a well. The community now has easy access to clean water for their families.

Children clad in their brand-new t-shirts during our annual Camp Espoir, together with their proud parents.

One of the subjects taught during Camp Espoir is art that helps cultivate the children's creativity. Art is also a therapeutic form of helping children heal from trauma.

Clean water initiative in Goma, a city that has been devastated by recent volcanic eruptions. The land in most villages around Goma is covered by ash and dust, giving it a blackened appearance.

Rolling green hills and sprawling tea plantations serve as the backdrop for a school for Pygmies in Tshibati.

My siblings and I with our inspiration, our everything, Maman.

Acknowledgments

My parents Victor and Pauline:
Thank you for teaching us to live beyond ourselves.

My siblings Denise, Rose, Joelle and Deo:
You have been my friends and partners since day one.
This is your story too.

My late brother Pierre:
Rest in peace.

Vernon and Lucille Vest:
I will forever be thankful for your love and support.

Pam and Wendell Lovewell:
Thank you for adopting me in your heart.

**Rick and Tammy, Misty and Jeff, Russ and Myrna,
Barret and Shannon, Dave and Jenny:**
Thank you for being my family.

Grace Mbuthia:
Thank you for being part of this adventure from day one.

My editors John Hunter, Myrna Moser and Tola Ferris:
Thank you!

Patrice Tsague and Nehemiah Project International Ministries:
Thank you for giving me the opportunity to tell my story.

Abigail Peter:
Thank you for all your hard work and dedication that made
this possible. It was a blessing working with you.

**All those who support the work of Mwangaza International
in the Democratic Republic of Congo:**
Thank you for inspiring me. This is your story too.

Join our battle for hope in the Democratic Republic of the Congo with Mwangaza International:

www.mwangazaint.org

Purchase the e-book at
50% OFF
with the promo code: INVP5FF

A Ministry of Nehemiah Project International

ABOUT THE PUBLISHER

Nehemiah Publishing is an exclusive full-service publisher operated by Nehemiah Project International Ministries. Our mission is to produce and distribute kingdom-class content that enables us to build kingdom businesses globally.

Our services include:
- Writing and editing
- Cover design and illustrations
- ISBN and copyright registration
- Book layout and design
- Book marketing and distribution
- Printing
- Fulfillment
- Translation
- Author consultation and coaching

Book formats:
- Paperback
- Hardcover
- E-Book
- Audio Book
- Flash Drives

We are an exclusive publisher, hence, we only take on authors whose work is consistent with our mission and vision. To be considered for our services, please visit us at **NehemiahPublishing.com** and fill out a publishing services request form.

ABOUT NEHEMIAH PROJECT

Nehemiah Project International Ministries, Inc. is a business development and support organization that works in partnership with churches, marketplace ministries, educational institutions, associations, and individuals around the world. We provide comprehensive, transformational, Bible-based business education, training, and business coaching for Christian entrepreneurs and organizations.

MISSION

To build kingdom businesses globally.

VISION

To transform the marketplace with
the gospel of the Lord Jesus Christ one
entrepreneur at a time.

TRAINING   COACHING   ACCESS TO CAPITAL

For more information, visit us at **NehemiahProject.org**.

BIBLICAL
ENTREPRENEURSHIP
Principles | Practices | Planning

A proven system that thousands of entrepreneurs around the world have used to align their business with their values, increase their top and bottom line while making a kingdom impact.

We use our proprietary course materials along with some of the best business resources available.

PRINCIPLES	**PRACTICES**	**PLANNING**
Ground your business in biblical truth	Best business practices for efficiency and growth	Develop a growth plan that aligns your mission, values, and goals with your kingdom impact

- Identifying Opportunities
- Taking Calculated Risks
- Biblical Profit
- Biblical Economics
- Marketing and Sales from a Biblical Approach

- Innovation
- Biblical Management
- Business Financing
- Succession and Exit
- Developing a Kingdom Business Plan

For more information or to enroll, visit us at **BE-Executive.com**.

OTHER COURSES

For more information, visit us at **NehemiahProject.org**.

KINGDOM
BUSINESS COACHING

Kingdom Business Coaching™ (KBC) is the sister company of Nehemiah Project. KBC is an international business coaching and consulting practice that uses a proactive 360-degree coaching approach with various strategic tools and experienced coaches to help clients build healthy God-honoring relationships, build kingdom companies that align with their values, and grow their top and bottom line with kingdom impact.

OUR MISSION

Helping kingdom companies achieve transformational results.

OUR SERVICES

 Ask a Kingdom Business Coach

 Group Coaching

 Customized Coaching

 Elite Coaching

COACHING SYSTEM

Business Life Cycle	Scorecard	KBC Keys	Team Development
Strategy Development	Marketing & Sales	Systems & Innovation	Financial Development

For more information or to schedule a free initial consultation, visit us at **KingdomBizCoaching.com**.

The **Global Kingdom Investors Network™** (GKIN) is an online investment matching service for qualified members of the Nehemiah E-Community™ who desire to raise debt or equity financing to grow their company. The goal of the network is to connect Biblical Entrepreneurs to kingdom impact investors and kingdom impact investors to quality, kingdom impact deals.

The GKIN hosts live and online Investors Forums with the purpose to introduce Biblical Entrepreneurs to investors and investors to kingdom impact opportunities.

For more information on how to raise money for your business or how to invest in kingdom companies visit our website: **GlobalKingdomInvesting.com**

NEHEMIAH E-COMMUNITY

Connecting
Biblical
Entrepreneurs
to resources,
and investors
to Kingdom
impact
opportunities

| LEARN | COACHING | CONNECT | COMMERCE | ACCESS FINANCING |

The Nehemiah Entrepreneurship Community (E-Community™) is a comprehensive and robust online membership platform, providing entrepreneurs with quality biblically-integrated online business training, group coaching, and opportunities to connect and network with other Biblical Entrepreneurs from around the world who share their values. The E-Community™ allows access to investors through a Global Kingdom Investors Network™. The E-Community™ is a secure, shared-value, high-impact network of investors and entrepreneurs who provide innovative products and services, and are contributing to the transformation of communities and nations.

"Staying connected with my entrepreneur friends from around the world through the E-Community strengthened me." - René Villar

For more information, visit **www.n-ecommunity.com**.

OTHER RESOURCES

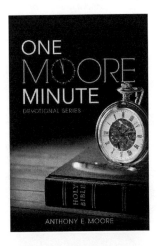